SLEEPING GIANT

kenny luck

CORE TEAM EXPERIENCE
WRITTEN BY BRIAN GASS

D1541510

LifeWay Press®
Nashville, Tennessee

AUTHOR:
Kenny Luck

**EDITORIAL
PROJECT LEADER:**
Brian Daniel

ART DIRECTOR:
Christi Kearney

GRAPHIC DESIGNER:
Susan Browne

CONTENT EDITORS:
Brian Gass
Gena Rogers

PRODUCTION EDITORS:
Juliana Duncan
Bethany McShurley

VIDEO DIRECTOR:
Frank Baker

VIDEO EDITOR:
Phil LeBeau

**DIRECTOR, LEADERSHIP
AND ADULT PUBLISHING:**
Bret Robbe

**MANAGING DIRECTOR,
LEADERSHIP AND
ADULT PUBLISHING:**
Bill Craig

Sleeping Giant Core Team Workbook
Published by LifeWay Press®
©2012 Kenny Luck

*kennyluck.com; everymanministries.com; facebook.com/KennyLuck;
twitter.com/kenny_luck*

All rights reserved. No part of this work may be reproduced, stored in a retrieval system or transmitted in any form or by any means, electronic or mechanical, including photocopying and recording, without express written permission of the publisher. Request for permission should be addressed to LifeWay Press®, One LifeWay Plaza, Nashville, TN 37234-0175.

ISBN: 978-1-4158-7204-8
Item: 005469853
Dewey Decimal Classification: 248.842
Subject Headings: MEN \ MINISTRY \ CHRISTIAN LIFE

Unless otherwise noted, all Scripture quotations are taken from the Holman Christian Standard Bible®, Copyright 1999, 2000, 2002, 2003 by Holman Bible Publishers. Used by permission. Scripture quotations marked NIV are taken from the Holy Bible, New International Version, copyright © 1973, 1978, 1984 by International Bible Society.

To order additional copies of this resource, order online at *www.lifeway.com/ kennyluck*; write LifeWay Men: One LifeWay Plaza, Nashville, TN 37234-0175; fax order to (615) 251-5933; call toll-free (800) 458-2772.

Printed in the United States of America

Leadership and Adult Publishing
LifeWay Church Resources
One LifeWay Plaza
Nashville, TN 37234-0175

Contents

About the Author   04

Introduction   05

The *Sleeping Giant* Experience   06

SESSION 01
  Waiting for a Hero   08

SESSION 02
  A Movement Begins with a Man   30

SESSION 03
  Mission, Vision, and Alignment   52

SESSION 04
  Strong Funnels and Pathways   74

SESSION 05
  Strong Relational Core and Groups   96

SESSION 06
  "Go" Time   118

Leader Notes   140

Group Covenant   156

Group Directory   157

About the Author

KENNY LUCK is the Men's Pastor at Saddleback Church in Lake Forest, California, where over 7,000 men are connected in small groups. He is also the Founder and President of Every Man Ministries which helps churches worldwide develop and grow healthy men's communities.

He is an ECPA Platinum Award Winning Author, who has written and coauthored 20 books, including *RISK, DREAM, FIGHT, SOAR, Every Man, God's Man, Every Young Man, God's Man,* and the *Every Man Bible Studies* from the best-selling *Every Man* Series.

Kenny is a trusted expert on men's issues. In addition to logging over 2 million miles in the air to speak to audiences, he has made numerous radio and television appearances that include ABC Family, Christian Broadcasting Network, and over 100 other programs worldwide. He has been a featured contributor to *SermonCentral.com, ChurchLeaders.com,* Rick Warren's *Ministry Toolbox, New Man, Men of Integrity, The Journal, HomeLife, Walk Thru the Bible,* and *Young Believers Magazine.*

So what does he think about all his private and personal achievements?

"None of this matters if my wife and children don't respect me as a man, husband, and father. ... They are my first ministry, and respect by others is meaningless without theirs. My relationships with them are the acid test of my life and ministry. So many parts of me are still broken, but God is healing me every day and I wake up every day in awe that His kingdom has come to me and comes through me. Every day I ask myself: *How did I get here?* When I speak I ask myself constantly, *What am I doing here?* or *How do I get to do what I do?* Absolutely none of it makes sense outside the grace of God."

Kenny is a graduate of UCLA where he met his wife, Chrissy. They have three children, Cara, Ryan, and Jenna, and live in Trabuco Canyon, California.

Follow Kenny on Facebook (*facebook.com/kennyluck*), on Twitter (*@kenny_luck*), and at *www.everymanministries.com.*

A Word from Kenny

DEAR PASTOR AND CORE TEAM, you are engaging this training because you get it. Healthy men change things at every level of society. You understand and see the reality that men have been given a mantle of influence that creates a large blast zone for better or for worse. You also see the victims of unhealthy men. Some of you have experienced that firsthand. Nowhere is this radius of impact more relevant than in the church. We are supposed to be reaching cultural man and producing leaders who support the kingdom mission and vision in local communities alongside their pastors. In that process, we are to be empowering health at all levels of society. But society is asking, "Where have all the good men gone?"

Sleeping Giant is going to attack the root of the problem.

This pathway for men's ministry has as its goal waking the Sleeping Giant—turning affiliated men in the church into activated men, moving men from the audience to the army and from being unintentional to intentional. Instead of skimming the surface of the water to limit the damage of the current moral and spiritual oil spill polluting communities, *Sleeping Giant* is going to cap the spill at its source. The church is going to become a center of masculine transformation and greatness. This is how the church was conceived and this will be its legacy again.

God has called every pastor worldwide to advance the kingdom of God in the community He has selected them to reach. God has also called the men of that body of believers to help Him. The *Sleeping Giant* strategy is the biblical way to implement and execute that vision. As you work together toward this goal, God is going to move mightily in your midst. As you pray and train together, God will create a powerful unit of God's men capable of attracting other men. By trusting God together and following the biblical directions laid out in the *Sleeping Giant* model, you will build the leadership engine that your church and community so desperately need. You are going to see men Get In, Get Healthy, Get Strong, and Get Going.

Know this: you will be fiercely opposed. Just as Moses walked out of Egypt with Pharaoh's work force, you are going after the one group Satan invests a great deal of effort and resources to control—men. Begin this battle with prayer and bathe all strategy in prayer. Lay down strong blankets of suppressive fire and guard your own heart. Then march together toward your victory.

The world is waiting for us to rise,

Kenny

The *Sleeping Giant* Experience

WELCOME TO A SIX-WEEK JOURNEY INTO *SLEEPING GIANT*! HERE'S HOW THE TRAINING WORKS:

INTRODUCTION // Each session begins with a narrative overview of the weekly topic. You will want to read this to set the stage for your personal study and to establish context for your time with the Core Team.

WORK AT HOME // If you want to grow in faith and find out what it means to be part of awakening the Sleeping Giant, you will enjoy unpacking this challenging material and applying it to your own journey as God's man. Each session in this workbook contains four short "Work at Home" segments for you to read and write about during the week leading up to your Core Team meeting. You may choose to do one per day or settle in for a Saturday morning personal retreat. There is also a testimony for you to read that fleshes out the principles you've been studying in real time.

ENRICHMENT // Throughout the Work at Home segments, you will see boxes that guide you to further enrichment. These will involve additional reading material for those who want to go deeper or grow in a particular area of faith and practice, movie ideas that will personally challenge you, or internet resources that can be faith-stretching exercises. Participate in as many or as few of these as God leads you.

CORE TEAM EXPERIENCE // Men appreciate getting together to hear each other's opinions, share some laughs, study the Word, encourage one another, and pray. Each week, your Core Team experience will begin with a review to get everyone on the same page. Next, you'll watch a video message from Kenny Luck and interact with questions for group discussion. (Discussion will be best if everyone has completed the Work at Home segments.) There is also an activity and/or Bible study in each Core Team experience that will help lay the foundation for your intentional men's ministry. You'll wrap up each meeting by summarizing key points and praying together.

ADDITIONAL ENCOURAGEMENT

This workbook includes ample space for you to write your answers, comments, and questions. A Notes page follows each session. This is where you can write any ideas, conclusions, challenges, and personal insights that you found meaningful that week.

This study is designed to cover a six-week time frame. However, if it takes you longer to complete the study personally or as a Core Team, take all the time you need. It is not unusual for a group to spend two or three meetings completing one lesson. Always go for depth over distance.

One last thing: Before you begin each session, commit your time to God. Ask the Holy Spirit to illumine your mind, guide your heart, and energize your spirit as you read each section and answer each question. Above all, adapt this study so that it truly works for you. Follow His leadership. This is your invitation to know God better, your opportunity to explore what a more passionate devotion to God means, and your encouragement to do this together with other God's men.

WAITING FOR A
HERO

Gotham is in trouble. A pervasive sickness has fallen across the land, evil has the upper hand, and the people are desperate for leadership— someone to make things better and heal wounds brought by merciless men and unsavory thugs. But who? Who will make things right? Who will bring justice? Who will give the bully a taste of his own medicine? Will the Dark Knight rise to save the day?

Hundreds of millions of dollars are spent as moviegoers seek to discover the answer to that question for the third time. We can't get enough of super heroes, but here's the problem: Hypothetical fantasy, which makes good-versus-evil movies reso- nate, now illustrates the real-life drama of our time. Unfortunately, mythic heroes with synthetic abs are not available to stop the bad guys. Real women and children in real communities oppressed by real evils wait for regular men like you, me, and the local mechanic to transform into a hero who delivers hope.

> "THE GOOD MAN BRINGS GOOD THINGS OUT OF THE GOOD STORED UP IN HIM, THE EVIL MAN BRINGS EVIL THINGS OUT OF THE EVIL STORED UP IN HIM."
>
> MATTHEW 12:35

But will men rise to the occasion? Will good men take a stand? Will God's men answer the call?

In this session, Core Team members will awaken to their context for men's ministry.

ON THE FOLLOWING PAGES, YOU WILL FIND SEVERAL PERSONAL STUDY SECTIONS TO READ AND THINK ABOUT BEFORE YOUR CORE TEAM MEETING. YOU ARE ALSO ENCOURAGED TO ANSWER THE QUESTIONS AND JOURNAL IN THE SPACE PROVIDED.

Broken Male Culture

We all know a guy who represents broken male culture. He might be like one of the beer commercial actors who comes off as so effeminate that the other macho guys in the scene mock him as they make plain that life can't get any better than making it to the bottom of a nice cold one. Or he could be like some TV personalities who think themselves "winning" when everyone knows otherwise. But perhaps the most representative figure of broken male culture is the deputy in *Courageous* who realizes that his life goal has been to be "good enough" as a husband, father, and man. For most of us, one of these descriptions may hit just a little too close to home.

What makes these distortions more painful is realizing the impact such men have on others around them. Broken-culture men are like sticks of dynamite that can go off, producing massive collateral damage. They self-preserve, self-protect, self-indulge, and seek to be self-important even at the expense of others. This powerful and dangerous acting out disappoints a loving Father who watches His sons expectantly, desiring that healthy expressions of character flow from them into the lives of others. Scripture tells us that the blast zones of broken male character and conduct break God's heart and boil His blood.

LESSONS FROM THE BIG SCREEN. Watch *Courageous*. Consider how these men's blast zones became an impact for good. Consider the other blast zones of influence in the film as well.

> *"The vineyard of the Lord Almighty is the nation of Israel, and the men of Judah are the garden of his delight. And he looked for justice, but saw bloodshed; for righteousness, but heard cries of distress."* Isaiah 5:7, NIV

1. The second part of verse 7 paints a terrible picture. How does this picture illustrate the world we live in while God's man sleeps? What are some examples of injustice, bloodshed, and cries of distress that come to mind? What role have men played in causing this pain?

2. Describe a typical vineyard or garden. How do those places symbolize the world God wants to see? In what ways can awakened men contribute to cultivating that kind of world?

Black Velvet

I was dazzled when I went to the jeweler to buy a diamond for my wife's engagement ring. As the jeweler popped open his briefcase, I expected to see a small bag holding a few diamonds preselected just for me. But after he placed a black velvet place mat on the table in front of me, I was stunned to see him pour out tens of thousands of dollars worth of diamonds. Against that black velvet I could see every cut and every facet of each gem. The contrast was remarkable and necessary to display the diamonds' glory.

The backdrop of our world is black
- 163 million orphans worldwide[1]
- 38.6 million global HIV cases[2]
- 27 million modern-day slaves[3]
- 2 million sexually trafficked children[4]
- 11.5 million single mothers in the U.S. alone[5]

Against this backdrop God wants to pour out His diamonds: men who'll love Him through their actions, shining hope into a hurting world. Let's look at one picture Jesus gave of our potential to impact the world rightly—to foster a culture of life rather than death, light instead of darkness.

> *"You are the salt of the earth. But if the salt should lose its taste, how can it be made salty? It's no longer good for anything but to be thrown out and trampled on by men. You are the light of the world. A city situated on a hill cannot be hidden." Matthew 5:13-14*

READ FOR YOURSELF

"Why Men Are In Trouble"
by William J. Bennett
(www.*cnn.com*)

"The End of Men"
by Hanna Rosin in
The Atlantic Monthly
(www.*theatlantic.com*)

"Men's Lib"
by Andrew Romano and
Tony Dokoupil in *Newsweek*
(www.*thedailybeast.com*)

3. Jesus used the image of salt to describe the need for a preserving influence in this world of decay. What examples of decay most disturb you? Which ones have the most impact in your community? Explain.

4. Jesus calls men to shine like diamonds against the backdrop of a very dark world. In what ways have you seen men impacting their world for good? How can you and your church be more involved as a force for good?

1. "UNICEF Progress for Children: A Report Card on Child Protection," no. 8, September 2009.
2. *Global Report: UNAIDS Report on the Global AIDS Epidemic,* 2010.
3. Andrew Cockburn, "21st Century Slaves," *National Geographic,* September 2003.
4. "UNICEF Progress for Children: A Report Card on Child Protection," no. 8, September 2009.
5. 2009 U.S. Census Bureau Report.

The Church Is Naked

Hans Christian Anderson once told a simple tale of two salesmen who convince the emperor that they have magical cloth only the wise can see. Not wanting to appear unwise himself, the emperor commissions them to make him a suit of clothes fit for royalty. Then the story gets purposefully uncomfortable. While the emperor cannot see the cloth himself, he pretends he can out of fear of appearing stupid. One bad decision follows another as everyone supports his denial. The painfully humiliating turning point is when the new "suit" is finished. The tailors pretend to dress the emperor, attending to every delusional detail before he proudly marches in a parade before his subjects who energetically join in the fantasy—that is, until one boy has the courage to shout, "The emperor has no clothes!" Appearance collides with reality.

The church has long lived in denial of a similar, serious problem. We continue the procession of appearances, focusing on a seemingly healthy church with successful weekend services, discipleship programs, and different ministries and outreaches to our credit. But often we mask the deep and abiding reality that no one wants to say out loud: the men of our congregations are affiliated but not activated, in the audience but not in the army.

AFFILIATED MAN
- I am not really needed.
- I am not being developed.
- I can't see where I fit in.
- I feel more welcome outside the church.
- The church is mainly for women and children.

ACTIVATED MAN
- This church needs me.
- I am becoming better here.
- I see where I fit in.
- I feel accepted and welcome here.
- Men are leading in the church.

"For where your treasure is, there your heart will be also.
The eye is the lamp of the body. If your eyes are healthy, your
whole body will be full of light. But if your eyes are unhealthy,
your whole body will be full of darkness. If then the light
within you is darkness, how great is that darkness!"
Matthew 6:21-23, NIV

5. This passage is about where we place our investment. Where is your church currently placing most of its treasure, time, energy, and passion?

6. How do you think a congregation of activated men could impact ongoing ministry and other areas of church life that currently seem to get more attention? How can activated men make things better?

High Value Targets

High value targets. This is what a sniper sees nestled in the cross-hairs of his high precision rifle. When I read the book *Point of Impact* by Stephen Hunter I was immersed in the world of the sniper for the first time. I was fascinated by the way these men's minds were trained to work and I was amazed at the parallels to Satan's assault on the church. The whole idea of a sniper reducing the enemy's fighting ability by striking at high value targets (especially officers) was certainly memorable. The goal: maximum disruption to enemy operations. Target leaders. Pin down. Demoralize.

For a sniper, rank is synonymous with influence. And when it comes to our topic of the church, men, and their capacity to deliver help or harm, Satan is no fool. In fact, the Bible warns of a savvy Enemy, lying in wait specifically for men, capitalizing on their ignorance of his proximity and presence to take them down. In the process, the man is neutralized, people around him suffer, and the church's best potential leaders are carried away from God's purposes, conformed to a pattern of broken male culture in the world. What is shocking is the willingness of churches to view men in the community as acceptable losses.

> *"Therefore my people will go into exile for lack of understanding; those of high rank will die of hunger and the common people will be parched with thirst. Therefore Death expands its jaws, opening wide its mouth; into it will descend their nobles and masses with all their brawlers and revelers."*
> *Isaiah 5:13-14, NIV*

7. What are some ways you feel that the Enemy has specifically targeted the men of your church?

8. Isaiah said "common people will be parched with thirst." For what do you see the people of your church thirsting as a result of men being sniped?

// **TESTIMONY** // "BLEACHER GUY"

Meet Paul. He is the proverbial man on the sidelines. Paul sat in the bleachers of Saddleback Church for seven years. He thought about all the things, carried around all the feelings, and fought all the internal battles we have mentioned. The tip of his iceberg looked like this: ex-college football player, successful pharmaceutical sales executive, smooth talker, trainer, strong man-in-command. But below the water line he was that all-too-common blend of outward confidence whose eyes betray fear. Paul had fragmented family issues, identity issues connected to being adopted, acceptance issues, career transitions to overcome, and powerful negative emotions connected to them. After seven years of sitting on the bleachers, Paul was invited to come to our men's leadership community on Thursday mornings. The result?

Bleacher Guy was transformed.

Paul encountered mentors, messages, and models that passed his "sniff test." That gave God the opportunity to get under the waterline of Paul's life. Slowly but surely, the Lord began to transform Paul's fears into faith in a loving God who makes men secure enough to look beyond themselves. Paul caught God's vision for his life in the church and began to see the church's vision for the community. His experience was so complete that he wanted every next step toward true significance and leadership we could offer him. Today Paul is Men's Director at one of our regional campuses and has led hundreds of men through that same life-transforming process.

What is your testimony?

How can you encourage other
men to leave the bleachers?

CORE TEAM MEETING

REVIEW

Welcome to our group time for *Sleeping Giant*! Hopefully you are looking forward to sharing life with the men of your Core Team and learning to lead other men to follow Christ passionately. Here are a few questions to help us review the week as well as begin participating in the group conversation.

1. When you first heard the title *Sleeping Giant*, what came to mind?

2. What are your personal goals for this study? What do you hope to learn about yourself or God and His kingdom?

3. What came to mind this week regarding where the Enemy is targeting the men in your church? What solutions is God beginning to stir in your heart?

▶ In this video teaching session, Kenny establishes the context for why we need a strong movement of God among men. Listen carefully as he reminds us of the importance of men for the church and for the world. We'll unpack this together after the video.

Watch Video Session 1:

"WAITING FOR A HERO" *(29:00)*

- The _____ of men are at the center of most suffering.

- Broken male culture is the _____ of modern journalism.

- Men are being called by God into a movement of _____ and _____.

- The hope of the world is the local _____.

- If the men of our churches are not _____, the churches are not _____.

⏸ Review your notes from the video teaching and answer the following questions together.

1. Kenny said that broken male culture is the wallpaper of journalism. What examples of that can you give?

2. If indeed the hope of the world is the church and the hope of the church is God's men, how bright does the future look to you? What gives you cause for hope?

3. Kenny gave several examples of Jesus standing up for people and administering justice. Which of these examples most moved you? Why?

FOLLOW KENNY
On Twitter: @Kenny_Luck
Facebook.com/KennyLuck

IF YOU MISSED THIS WEEK'S VIDEO VISIT
LIFEWAY.COM/SLEEPINGGIANT TO CATCH UP.

CORE TEAM ACTIVITY

Church and Parachurch: A Marriage Made in Heaven

Consider a men's event that your church has hosted or one that you have attended. If not a men's event specifically, consider another churchwide event or campaign and how it might relate to men. Break into small groups and discuss together.

1. What were the strengths of this event? What made it attractive to men?

2. What were the drawbacks to the event or things that might have turned men off?

3. How did your church ride the wave of momentum from the event and follow up?

4. How could you have done a better job of that?

If your church is like most local churches, you've been exposed to Christian, faith-based events with mixed results. At times the relationship seems competitive; at other times their work has seemed obsolete. God has often inspired such movements, though, with the intent of growing His local churches. Here are some questions to ask when your church considers working alongside other men's ministries on a similar mission. It would be helpful to answer these questions together before an event:

- What are the core values and vision of your church?

- What has God called you to do here in your community?

- What initiatives do you have that need energy and muscle?

- How can the men of our church help support what God has called you to do?

- Where is leadership most desperately needed?

- Would you be open to getting men connected, healthy, strong and going into those areas of need through the local church?

As your church begins to develop an overall strategy for activating men, the answers to these questions will guide you—whether you're focusing on your church's men's ministry or looking to partner with others in your community.

CORE TEAM BIBLE STUDY

On the next few pages, you will find Scriptures to read and questions to discuss that will help your Core Team further develop an effective biblical philosophy for a movement of God's men. Read the Scripture and discuss together.

"For what makes everything clear is light. Therefore it is said: Get up, sleeper, and rise up from the dead, and the Messiah will shine on you."
Ephesians 5:14

1. In what ways do you see men as sleeping giants in your church? If they were to be awakened, how would it impact your church? Your community?

If a movement of men is to begin in your church, cultural man must become God's man. This process begins with your Core Team.

"Do not be conformed to this age, but be transformed by the renewing of your mind, so that you may discern what is the good, pleasing, and perfect will of God." Romans 12:1-2

2. A fine line exists between being cross-cultural to reach men for Christ and becoming too cultural. What does your church do to move men's allegiance away from the world and toward God?

If we are to see our communities changed for Christ, men will need more than a program. They will need to be transformed and inspired to move from the audience to active duty. That's a heavy burden to carry, but you are not alone. Your Core Team will lead by example.

> "'What you're doing is not good,' Moses' father-in-law said to him. 'You will certainly wear out both yourself and these people who are with you, because the task is too heavy for you. You can't do it alone. Now listen to me; I will give you some advice, and God be with you. You be the one to represent the people before God and bring their cases to Him. Instruct them about the statutes and laws, and teach them the way to live and what they must do. But you should select from all the people able men, God-fearing, trustworthy, and hating bribes. Place them over the people as commanders of thousands, hundreds, fifties, and tens. They should judge the people at all times. Then they can bring you every important case but judge every minor case themselves. In this way you will lighten your load, and they will bear it with you. If you do this, and God so directs you, you will be able to endure, and also all these people will be able to go home satisfied.'"
> Exodus 18:17-23

3. Jethro, Moses' father-in-law, helped him become a more effective leader and solved one of the real problems the community faced— activating the capable men. Describe the men waiting to be activated in your church. What are their strengths and weaknesses?

"Moses listened to his father-in-law and did everything he said. So Moses chose able men from all Israel and made them leaders over the people as commanders of thousands, hundreds, fifties, and tens. They judged the people at all times; they would bring the hard cases to Moses, but they would judge every minor case themselves." Exodus 18:24-26

4. Talk about ways Jethro's approach to ministry helped Moses. How might this approach help your Core Team and your pastor?

Church leaders can't accomplish alone the tasks to which God calls them. As churches continue to pour massive amounts of resources into programs and staff, a network of men who could accomplish the same things more effectively lies dormant.

"If you were of the world, the world would love you as its own. However, because you are not of the world, but I have chosen you out of it, the world hates you." John 5:19

Our negligence to reach out to men and inspire them to lead is always Satan's gain. The men of the church too often become a muscle that doesn't get used. That's why the church must press hard to win the battle for men's souls, encouraging them to be Christ-followers not just in name, but in daily service to Him.

5. In what ways does the church allow God's man to look more like cultural man? What role do you think Satan plays in this?

"For just as through one man's disobedience the many were made sinners, so also through the one man's obedience the many will be made righteous." Romans 5:19

6. Consider the blast zones emanating from Adam and Christ, the two men mentioned in this passage. How might your church better mirror the latter?

"So the eye cannot say to the hand, 'I don't need you!' Or again, the head can't say to the feet, 'I don't need you!'" 1 Corinthians 12:21

7. How does your church communicate that men are needed and valued as leaders? How might your church better validate the men who serve?

For too long the church has communicated to men that their presence is appreciated but not really needed. In truth, men are seeking purpose, significance, legacy, and validation. If the church does not provide these things, men will find them outside the church, within the broken culture.

"Jesus called them over and said to them, 'You know that those who are regarded as rulers of the Gentiles dominate them, and their men of high positions exercise power over them. But it must not be like that among you. On the contrary, whoever wants to become great among you must be your servant, and whoever wants to be first among you must be a slave to all. For even the Son of Man did not come to be served, but to serve, and to give His life—a ransom for many.'" Mark 10:42-45

8. Jesus does not neglect the needed influence of men in this passage. How does Jesus redefine their power to influence others?

If we pour our lives into developing the men in our churches, guiding them into strong moral and spiritual pathways, a shallow cultural vision will fall by the wayside. Men will stand up as God's men and will change the world for good.

WRAP

- Behaviors of men fuel cultural suffering.
- Transformed men reduce suffering and become culturally relevant.
- God's man must be distinguishable from cultural man.
- The goal is to have healthier leaders and healthier churches through activating the affiliated.
- A vision of a better future and a clear pathway will capture the imaginations of men.
- Satan's primary targets are leaders and complacent, unsuspecting men.
- Men need a place to express what they have experienced through other Christian, faith-based events. The best place for that is the local church.
- Strong moral and spiritual pathways will guide men away from shallow cultural vision.

PRAY TOGETHER

NEXT WEEK

[ ] Read session introduction on page 31

[ ] Complete Work at Home study

[ ] Review enrichment options

[ ] Read *Sleeping Giant* chapters 5-8 (optional)

FOLLOW KENNY

On Twitter: @Kenny_Luck
Facebook.com/KennyLuck

A MOVEMENT BEGINS WITH A MAN

One man can make a huge difference; he can begin a movement that will change the world. Take, for example, the fictitious story of Charles Xavier—better known as Professor X in the popular *X-Men* series. Xavier believes so strongly that mutants can impact the world for good that he intently searches for all he can find. Once he locates these gifted individuals, he brings them back to his manor and trains them to handle coming conflicts. Charles Xavier understands the powerful influence that one man—not to mention a small group of well-trained superheroes—can wield against the darkness.

Every man's life has a blast zone: he will shake the world either for evil or for good. That's why it's so important for each man to realize the importance of being responsible. He must consider the impact his actions will have on others.

The character, conduct, and choices of two men, Adam and Christ, represent the choice that lies before us all. Either we will be like Adam, bringing death to our relationships with God and people; or we will be like Christ, bringing life to all those in our spheres of influence.

> "SINCE BY THE ONE MAN'S TRESPASS, DEATH REIGNED THROUGH THAT ONE MAN, HOW MUCH MORE WILL THOSE WHO RECEIVE THE OVERFLOW OF GRACE AND THE GIFT OF RIGHTEOUSNESS REIGN IN LIFE THROUGH THE ONE MAN, JESUS CHRIST."
>
> ROMANS 5:17

Throughout Scripture God emphasizes men as the chief influencers and agents of His plans in this world. In virtually every story in the Bible that follows the fall, God selects men to lead in the midst of darkness. He gives them a vision, surrounds them with an infrastructure of supporting leadership, and uses them to bring health and growth to the community of faith. This pattern was never better modeled than through the life of Christ.

In this session, Core Team members will learn and assume their roles of leadership in the church and community.

ON THE FOLLOWING PAGES, YOU WILL FIND SEVERAL PERSONAL STUDY SECTIONS TO READ AND CONSIDER BEFORE YOUR CORE TEAM MEETING. YOU ARE ALSO ENCOURAGED TO ANSWER THE QUESTIONS AND JOURNAL IN THE SPACE PROVIDED.

Men Are Responsible

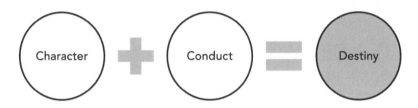

The Bible presents men as central, important instruments of divine movement. God has given us a powerful responsibility and accountability that should temper any male frustration with the current gender debates. But with our selection comes God's examination and investigation of our hearts and motives. Remember, God first called Adam—not Eve—on the carpet over their shared disobedience.

Similarly, God called Eli to account for the actions of his sons, not their mother. The Lord judged His leaders, His kings, and His priests harshly for mishandling their mantles of influence. Sometimes He even sent special envoys to address or, in many cases, dress down His men when their character and conduct displeased. Today God charges fathers with material, relational, and spiritual responsibility for the marriage and family. He even places "liens" on the prayers of men who fail to respect the privilege of their ordained position, refusing to hear men who fail to lead with compassion and justice.

LESSONS FROM THE BIG SCREEN. Watch one of the *X-Men* movies together or with your family. Consider what it took to begin the movement.

Compare this to what needs to happen in our churches.

"Husbands, in the same way, live with your wives with an understanding of their weaker nature yet showing them honor as coheirs of the grace of life, so that your prayers will not be hindered." 1 Peter 3:7

1. What do you think it means that wives have a "weaker nature" than their husbands? How has broken male culture misconstrued this concept?

2. Consider someone in your life who models consideration and respect. What difference does it seem to make in his life? Ask God to help that brother remain a strong model of His love.

Revelation and Response

Life is overwhelming.

In the middle of the cultural wars surrounding men, we need biblical confidence that appears lacking. We need direct revelation from God about who we are supposed to be and how we are supposed to act. Out of this will flow a new unity, identity, energy, and expression that will result in a powerful advance of God's purposes.

The start of your church's men's movement must begin with a burning bush encounter with God. How does He want you to relate to men in your congregation and community? Flowing from His revelation to you will come practical energy and a pursuit of God's will that sparks a men's movement that sees significant bursts of God's spoken and

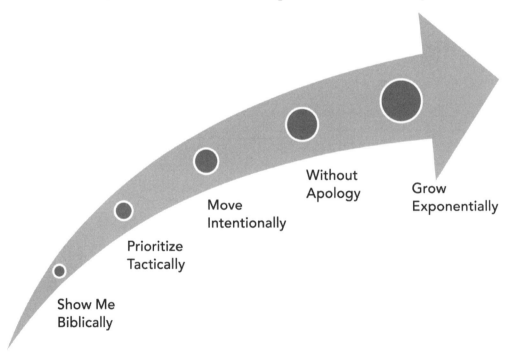

Show Me
Biblically

Prioritize
Tactically

Move
Intentionally

Without
Apology

Grow
Exponentially

active will and leans on Him for spiritual, material, physical, and emotional energy to carry out His plans. Listen as the apostle Paul encourages his son in the faith, Timothy, with biblical knowledge and a strategy for success.

> *"What you have heard from me in the presence of many witnesses, commit to faithful men who will be able to teach others also."* 2 Timothy 2:2

3. Consider what you know of Paul's teaching to the church in his epistles, and particularly to his young church planters and pastors. What kinds of revelations do you think Timothy remembered and strove to pass on?

4. Which men in your church might qualify as "faithful men … able to teach others"? What traits do they share? Why is each man important in the context of God's plan or pattern?

READ FOR YOURSELF

The Master Plan for Evangelism
by Robert E. Coleman

The Man God Uses
by Henry T. Blackaby and Tom Blackaby

The Purpose-Driven Life: What on Earth Am I Here for? by Rick Warren

Abraham's 318

Adam failed to lead properly, but this story from Abraham's early life shows just how effectively a man might meet challenges.

> *"When Abram heard that his relative had been taken prisoner, he assembled his 318 trained men, born in his household, and they went in pursuit as far as Dan. And he and his servants deployed against them by night, attacked them, and pursued them as far as Hobah to the north of Damascus. He brought back all the goods and also his relative Lot and his goods, as well as the women and other people."*
> Genesis 14:14-16

Abraham's reaction to the news that four evil leaders had ransacked his nephew's city, looted its goods, and enslaved its citizens is impressive. The bad guys had no idea Lot had an uncle who could rain thunder and strike with lightning force with a mere 318 helpers. Abraham pulled off a nighttime raid with a precision attack and gave a dominating physical performance. All men who love their families, love justice, and love against-all-odds stories want to shout, "Go, Abraham!" But this account is included in Scripture as more than just an exciting story. More impressive is the implied strength of Abraham's leadership ability.

5. Reread verse 14. Think about the men in your church who might fill a leadership role. What are you doing to train them (and yourself) for moments when a specific battle must be fought?

6. Who in your community is currently held hostage by the Enemy and would benefit from the intervention of an army of well-trained men marshaled for battle? How would this benefit your church and community?

LEADERSHIP LESSONS FROM ABRAHAM'S STORY

- Be in total command.
- Intentionally invest in and train men.
- Be able to assemble men who suit up and show up.
- Raise up men in your own household.
- Know how to skillfully deploy men for victory.
- Be ready to respond powerfully and forcefully at a moment's notice.

David's Network

King David provided an example of how to build a network of men for implementing the vision that God gives your church.

> *"David assembled all the leaders of Israel in Jerusalem: the leaders of the tribes, the leaders of the divisions of the king's service, the commanders of thousands and the commanders of hundreds, and the officials in charge of all the property and cattle of the king and his sons, along with the court officials, the fighting men, and all the brave warriors. Then King David rose to his feet and said, 'Listen to me, my brothers and my people. It was in my heart to build a house as a resting place for the ark of the Lord's covenant ... I made plans to build.'"* 1 Chronicles 28:1-2

7. Notice the layers of leadership David had on hand to help him fulfill a vision. What specific vision might your church fulfill with enough manpower? How could you help such a force accomplish that God-sized vision?

8. Read the rest of 1 Chronicles 28 from your Bible. Then see the chart on building a network of men. How does David's method reflect each step?

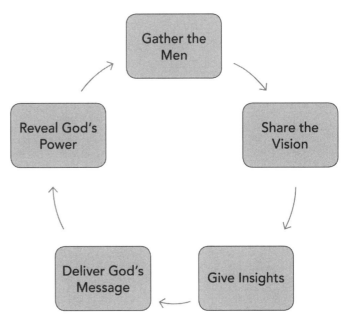

Big visions amount to little without big muscle behind them. David, a God's man with extraordinary vision, had a network of men supporting him. Through integrity, example, and structure, David made certain to surround himself with strong leaders who worked as his operational foundation. God put this structural leadership account in the Bible so that other godly leaders would see it, marvel at it, imitate it, and strive to implement it in order to fulfill the vision God gives them.

BUILDING A NETWORK

- Summon the men.
- Share the vision.
- Strengthen the men.
- Select leaders.
- Strengthen the leaders with the support of other leaders.

// **TESTIMONY** // MISSIONS IN CHINA

John works among an unreached people group in China. Early in his ministry days and outreach efforts there, John could already see what a challenge the field would present. The Chinese people risked much in listening to the gospel of Jesus, and they stood to lose much indeed if they decided to follow Christ. Evangelism was and still is illegal in that country, so the potential for a powerful movement of God among the house churches in John's province seemed like too much to hope for.

To some degree the believers in this particular Chinese city were lulled into a sense of passivity, largely due to the strong arm of the government. While they loved to study the Bible, they were reticent to share. They would sit for hours, soak in the teaching, and sing praises to God for what He had done in their lives; but John wanted to help the believers become more aggressive in sharing their faith and teaching the Bible to others. So he decided to try a less passive approach to teaching.

John began using a method very similar to the "show-how" method that Kenny will describe in his video message this week. John would read a small portion of Scripture to a small group of men, and then he would train them for at least an hour to make sure they understood it. Next they would practice teaching one another in the same manner. When they felt confident with the material, John prayed for them and sent them out to train five others just as they had been trained. As a result, every man became a minister; the churches in John's province began to grow exponentially.

Describe a time when someone showed you how to do something and helped you do it.

What lessons from John's approach can you apply in your church setting?

CORE TEAM MEETING

REVIEW

As you begin your group time together this week, here are a few questions to help start your group discussion.

1. Which biblical figure studied this week made the biggest impact on your thinking about working with men? Why?

2. Consider the women and children you know. How have you seen them negatively impacted by men who did not understand their own responsibility before God? How have you seen them positively impacted?

3. How has God challenged you this week to be more active in leading your church and community toward Christ?

In this video teaching session, Kenny gives biblical examples of movements of God among men. Listen carefully as he challenges us to be intentional about men's ministry. We'll unpack this together after the video.

Watch Video Session 2:
"A MOVEMENT BEGINS WITH A MAN" *(26:00)*

• Your _____ about men reflects your ministry to men.

• The church all over the world is struggling to deliver its mission _____.

• Jesus started with _____.

• Job one for Jesus: Start _____ men and fully _____ them.

• Jesus Christ practiced _____ men's ministry.

Review your notes from the video teaching and answer the following questions together.

1. Kenny contrasted Adam and Jesus in several ways. List and discuss the differences.

2. Describe Kenny's "show-how" method of training men. What do you think are the strengths of this method?

3. Kenny quotes Colossians 1:28-29, which reminds us that admonishing, teaching, and presenting play important roles in the discipleship process. How do these things work together to strengthen men for kingdom work?

FOLLOW KENNY
On Twitter: @Kenny_Luck
Facebook.com/KennyLuck

IF YOU MISSED THIS WEEK'S VIDEO VISIT **LIFEWAY.COM/SLEEPINGGIANT** TO CATCH UP.

CORE TEAM ACTIVITY

Vineyard of Hope

Read Isaiah 5:1-7 aloud. Then break into small groups to discuss it.

For the Israelites God provided a place of promise, abundant provision, and strong protection. There He planted His people like a vineyard, wanting them to take advantage of the amazing place of deliverance. He hoped that out of such a fertile context His people would produce "good grapes" (positive spiritual and character growth); but to His deep disappointment, He found only "bad fruit" among them.

1. Who was at fault in this situation?

2. Exactly what kind of fruit had God hoped to find?

3. To whom did God look as He tracked Israel's spiritual growth and health?

4. What does that reveal about God's purpose and pattern for His people?

5. How was the community of faith impacted by a lack of godly leadership?

6. What are the implications for your church, its leaders, and its men?

As you continue to work toward a thriving movement of God's men in your church and community, make sure you thank your heavenly Father for giving you fertile ground and helping cultivate it for your good and His glory.

CORE TEAM BIBLE STUDY

On the next few pages, you will find Scriptures to read and questions to discuss that will help your Core Team further develop an effective biblical philosophy for a movement of God's men. Read the Scripture and discuss together.

> "*Observe the words of this covenant and follow them, so that you will succeed in everything you do. All of you are standing today before the LORD your God—your leaders, tribes, elders, officials, all the men of Israel, your children, your wives, and the foreigners in your camps who cut your wood and draw your water.*" *Deuteronomy 29:9-11*

1. Think about the areas of your life where you most focus on success. What role do you think obedience to God's Word plays in determining true success? Explain.

Obedience breeds success. If men heed Moses' warning and follow God wholeheartedly, their blast radii will be littered with blessings and life for those around them. Men should feel responsible because they *are* responsible.

"Today I have set before you life and prosperity, death and adversity. For I am commanding you today to love the LORD your God, to walk in His ways, and to keep His commands, statutes, and ordinances, so that you may live and multiply, and the LORD your God may bless you in the land you are entering to possess. But if your heart turns away and you do not listen and you are led astray to bow down to other gods and worship them, I tell you today that you will certainly perish and will not live long in the land you are entering to possess across the Jordan." Deuteronomy 30:15-18

2. So much of the future rides on the obedience of men, including issues of life and prosperity. What are the cultural implications for your community as God's men choose to obey?

The choice laid before the children of Israel is just as real for us and just as urgent. We must choose today to be sons of Christ rather than sons of culture.

"Therefore My people will go into exile because they lack knowledge; her dignitaries are starving, and her masses are parched with thirst ... Therefore, as a tongue of fire consumes straw and as dry grass shrivels in the flame, so their roots will become like something rotten and their blossoms will blow away like dust, for they have rejected the instruction of the LORD of Hosts, and they have despised the word of the Holy One of Israel." Isaiah 5:13,24

3. Read Isaiah 5:13 and 24 above. In what ways are the men of your church living in spiritual and personal exile? Explain.

"If you return, Israel—this is the LORD's declaration—you will return to Me, if you remove your detestable idols from My presence and do not waver, then you can swear, 'As the LORD lives,' in truth, in justice, and in righteousness, then the nations will be blessed by Him and will pride themselves in Him. For this is what the LORD says to the men of Judah and Jerusalem: Break up the unplowed ground; do not sow among the thorns. Circumcise yourselves to the LORD; remove the foreskin of your hearts, men of Judah and residents of Jerusalem. Otherwise, My wrath will break out like fire and burn with no one to extinguish it because of your evil deeds."
Jeremiah 4:1-4

4. God calls us to return to Him when we are in exile. What decisions need to be made by your Core Team and the men of your church in order to turn to Him? What might you have to give up?

As a community, the men of Israel had detached themselves from covenant and abandoned responsibility because they were engaged in many cultural practices that were not honoring to God. Sadly, covenant men then and churched men now are not so different.

"How sad for me! For I am like one who—when the summer fruit has been gathered after the gleaning of the grape harvest—finds no grape cluster to eat, no early fig, which I crave. Godly people have vanished from the land; there is no one upright among the people. All of them wait in ambush to shed blood; they hunt each other with a net. Both hands are good at accomplishing evil: the official and the judge demand a bribe; when the powerful man communicates his evil desire, they plot it together." *Micah 7:1-3*

5. In what recent examples have you seen men—even Christian men—plotting together for evil? Explain the impact this had on you.

> *"I searched for a man among them who would repair the wall and stand in the gap before Me on behalf of the land so that I might not destroy it, but I found no one."* Ezekiel 22:30

6. The thought of God having to search for a faithful man to stand up for the land is sad. Which men in your church might be willing to "repair the wall" and "stand in the gap"? In what ways?

While it is easy to be discouraged by the blast zone of broken-cultured man, you must remember that God is at work among men in the kingdom and in your church. You can be agents of redemption.

> *"From the days of John the Baptist until now, the kingdom of heaven has been suffering violence, and the violent have been seizing it by force."* Matthew 11:12

7. In what ways does the kingdom of heaven suffer violence? What do you think it means for us to seize it by force?

For too long, men in the church have been collective bystanders. Men, it is past time for us to stand up and lead our families, our churches, and our communities to bear the standard for justice and goodness.

"Then he went on to Derbe and Lystra, where there was a disciple named Timothy, the son of a believing Jewish woman, but his father was a Greek. The brothers at Lystra and Iconium spoke highly of him. Paul wanted Timothy to go with him, so he took him and circumcised him because of the Jews who were in those places, since they all knew that his father was a Greek. As they traveled through the towns, they delivered the decisions reached by the apostles and elders at Jerusalem for them to observe. So the churches were strengthened in the faith and increased in number daily." Acts 16:1-5

8. Paul understood the important task of training men to advance the kingdom. How does Paul model the "show-how" method with young Timothy?

Paul understood the power and promise of men as well as the need to take advantage of their energies. Timothy, Silas, Luke, Mark, Titus, Epaphras, Tychicus, Onesimus, and Erastus were among the men Paul equipped. They became like their teacher, planting the first churches all over the Mediterranean.

WRAP

- Adam and Jesus made choices that led to two blast zones, each of which had very different results.
- The character and conduct of men have a profound influence on life and prosperity.
- People have suffered unjustly as a result of men's irresponsibility with what God has given them.
- The church must intentionally provide an environment to develop what God has already placed in every man.
- Living examples of great integrity, training, and commitment provide a foundation for men's ministry. These men are essential to the goal.
- The power of men comes from God's own revelation to man and requires great responsibility and response.
- Fully trained men, mentored by the well-discipled, are the key to transforming today's church for the Lord's purpose.

PRAY TOGETHER

NEXT WEEK

[ ] Read session introduction on page 53

[ ] Complete Work at Home study

[ ] Review enrichment options

[ ] Read *Sleeping Giant* chapters 9-10 (optional)

FOLLOW KENNY
On Twitter: @Kenny_Luck
Facebook.com/KennyLuck

MISSION, VISION, AND ALIGNMENT

In the National Football League a quarterback is always important. No one touches the football more than he does. No one is responsible for turning the ball over as often either. Even a game's time management rests on his shoulders lest the team pile up penalty yardage. The 2011-2012 NFL season perfectly illustrated just how important a quarterback's leadership is to the team: the perennial contender, the Indianapolis Colts, had to do without their future Hall-of-Fame quarterback, Peyton Manning. Without his strong leadership and skill under center, the team lost its sense of vision—not to mention almost every game!

Across the conference was another team whose quarterback played a similarly crucial role in their success. The Denver Broncos looked hapless for the first part of the season; then a quarterback considered not quite good enough as a passer to be successful at the professional level stepped on the field. From the time he broke the first huddle, Tim Tebow exuded leadership. He knew his team's abilities, and he believed that they could be champions. His confidence led the team to numerous last-second victories as his vision and desire to win infected the entire organization and resulted in a division title.

> "WITHOUT REVELATION PEOPLE RUN WILD, BUT ONE WHO LISTENS TO INSTRUCTION WILL BE HAPPY."
>
> PROVERBS 29:18

Just as a focused quarterback is crucial to a successful NFL team, the pastor who communicates the vision God has given him to a handful of skilled men proves vitally important. Men need a sense of mission in order to be effective in their communities. They need a vision to follow. They need inspiration to fall in behind their pastor as he leads the charge to advance the kingdom.

In this session, Core Team members will create a strong mission and vision statement for men's ministry that aligns with the vision of the pastor.

ON THE FOLLOWING PAGES, YOU WILL FIND SEVERAL PERSONAL STUDY SECTIONS TO READ AND CONSIDER BEFORE YOUR CORE TEAM MEETING. YOU ARE ALSO ENCOURAGED TO ANSWER THE QUESTIONS AND JOURNAL IN THE SPACE PROVIDED.

Magic Wand

In your group time this week, you'll have the opportunity to participate in a magic wand session as you get familiar with the concept and start brainstorming ideas meant to strengthen your men's ministry. The chart to the right shows some common responses to the question, "If you had a magic wand and could 'zap' the men's culture in your church, what would happen?"

This session is all about painting your target. To build a God-sized dream, begin with the end in mind. Fully invest in the process of creating meaningful mission and vision for your men's ministry. Most importantly, invite the Lord to give you His vision. Ask Him to help each leader have a personal buy-in and "skin in the game" where your church's outreach to men is concerned. Consider the chart to the right and the passage below as you prepare for your group meeting this week.

> "The LORD answered Moses: 'Bring Me 70 men from Israel known to you as elders and officers of the people. Take them to the tent of meeting and have them stand there with you. Then I will come down and speak with you there. I will take some of the Spirit who is on you and put the Spirit on them. They will help you bear the burden of the people, so that you do not have to bear it by yourself.'" Numbers 11:16-17

LESSONS FROM THE BIG SCREEN. Watch *Facing the Giants* together or with your family. Consider how one man's vision and passion can make a difference in both a team and a community.

1. Notice that God delivered His vision to Moses but commanded him to draw in other men to share the burden. How do you think this Core Team was able to help Moses carry out God's plan?

2. What is the Holy Spirit's role in leadership? What do you think the transfer of the Holy Spirit in this passage indicates?

The Magic Wand Whiteboard		
If you had a magic wand and could "zap" the men's culture in your church, what would happen? **"Our men would be** _____ **(fill in the blank)** _____**."**		
Connected to other men	Defeating temptations	Generous givers
Men of the Word	Sharing their faith	Supporting other ministries
Men of the Spirit	Men of prayer	Blessing the community
Great husbands	Behind vision of senior pastor	Helping the poor
Great dads	Making disciples	Planting needed ministries
More responsible	Spiritual leaders in homes	Leading small groups
Serving in the church	Coaching small group leaders	Helping pastor the people
Impacting the marketplace	An actionable network	Changing the world
Standing against injustice	Tithers	Reaching the broken
Donating skill sets to church	Trained for ministry	Fighting evil everywhere

Step 1: Clearly define the mission and vision of your men's ministry.

The magnetic drawing board toy I had as a child was called an Etch-A-Sketch. It was the iPad of its time for children and adults who couldn't contain their creative impulses. This thick red tablet had a milky white screen with two small knobs at the bottom that would move a black magnetic line up, down, and side-to-side. Those really adept with the knobs could create curving lines and some amazing pictures, but few had this skill because an Etch-A-Sketch only makes one continuous line. It doesn't allow stopping and placing the cursor in a new location on the screen. The only way to start fresh was to turn the tablet upside down, give it a shake, and voila—you got a new canvas!

As you develop your vision for men's ministry, plan to do a little Etch-A-Sketching of your own. Begin by developing a strong, clear vision. Often men fail to participate in men's ministry because they don't like to associate with things that don't reflect strength, excellence, and quality; therefore, a men's ministry that knows why it is there, is living out its mission and vision, and shows that it is committed to that vision will pass the first test most men use to gauge whether or not to be part of something. The vision, then, must foster deep relationships, intentional leader development, and spiritual health: the core values every men's ministry owes to its pastor and the men it serves. If those values are not deeply embedded in the leadership and culture of your men's ministry, do not expect the commitment, energy, fraternity, productivity, and transformations that accompany these factors when they are present.

"Do not remember the past events,
Pay no attention to things of old.
Look, I am about to do something new;
even now it is coming. Do you not see it?
Indeed, I will make a way in the wilderness,
rivers in the desert." Isaiah 43:18-19

3. In what ways does your church dwell on the past? How might that hinder your ministry moving forward?

4. God casts a bold vision for what He desires to create in the desert. What similarities do you see between Isaiah 43:18-19 and your hopes for your church's men's ministry?

READ FOR YOURSELF

Game Plan for Life: Your Personal Playbook for Success
by Joe Gibbs

Every Man, God's Man
by Stephen Arterburn, Kenny Luck, and Mike Yorkey

The Purpose-Driven Church by Rick Warren

57

Step 2: Be strongly aligned with the senior pastor.

Few things about ministry are worse than seeing a church self-destruct. As a men's pastor, the thought of God's men instigating disunity is particularly disturbing to me. Having consulted with hundreds of churches, I am all too familiar with the reality that some men's groups go rogue. The biggest failure of any men's group comes when its leaders desire the men's ministry's success over serving their pastor and making him successful.

The leaders of any group within a local church must remember that God called the pastor, the shepherd of the people, first. God speaks to the pastor about where He wants to take the body and places him in authority over those in his congregation. Our pastors are our leaders. The *Sleeping Giant* process directly connects the success of the men's ministry, its leaders, and those participating in it to the ministry traction it provides to the senior pastor. Remember, his success is your church's success.

> *"Remember your leaders who have spoken God's word to you. As you carefully observe the outcome of their lives, imitate their faith." Hebrews 13:7*

5. Think about a church leader who has made a tremendous impression on you or has invested in you. In what ways have you sought to imitate his faith?

6. Remember and consider your leaders. Sadly many men do the opposite: they forget and ignore. When have you seen this occur to the detriment of the church? Explain.

LESSONS IN LEADERSHIP

- A pastor calls men by name.
- A pastor communicates tribal knowledge uniquely meant for men.
- A pastor cultivates a personal connection with men.
- A pastor accumulates relational capital with men to spend later on strategic priorities.
- A pastor directly mobilizes the men to get things done rather than relying on the bulletin.
- A pastor positions men as spiritual leaders in the church.

A Pastor and His Men

Around the world courageous pastors hungry for new vitality and strength are choosing to build intentional men's ministries that reflect the character and thinking of the local church and seek to harness the men's process for that mission.

It is exciting to see men all over the globe forming ranks around their pastors, as those senior ministers value and include their men as vital to their success. As a result, men work together to ignite and accelerate kingdom works. The pride and fear that once crippled communities of men gives way to humility and faith. What emerges in churches is a stronger and unified *esprit de corps* that transcends the stale and useless status quo of the past. Evil has a reason to tremble at these developments in the body of Christ because unified God's men are synonymous with divine advances and manifestations of His presence.

> "How good and pleasant it is
> when brothers live together in harmony!
> It is like fine oil on the head,
> running down on the beard,
> running down on Aaron's beard,
> onto his robes.
> It is like the dew of Hermon
> falling on mountains of Zion.
> For there the LORD has appointed the blessing—
> life forevermore." Psalm 133

7. Think of a time when you saw men unified and working toward a common cause. Describe what that looked like.

8. Psalm 133 speaks of how the blessing of God trickles down from the man of God to his men and his community. How have you seen that trickle-down effect in action?

9. Review the sidebar and then discuss the concept of rogue men's groups. Why do you think they fail to bring about the unity God desires?

HOW TO IDENTIFY ROGUE MEN'S GROUPS:

- No defined goals
- No close pastoral supervision
- No willingness to change format to receive new believers
- Stagnant or declining growth
- Poor response to pastoral inquiry into what they are doing
- Talking-head teaching with knowledge focus
- No sending, service, or missions synergy with the church
- Unwillingness to modify format for church campaigns

// **TESTIMONY** // PASTORS AND THEIR MEN

A pastor in Tennessee calls his men to the altar for prayer every Sunday before the sermon begins. Those in the balcony kneel at their seats as they all pray for the lost and for their families.

What do you think this simple act communicates to the church?

A pastor in California always meets with the men of his church before announcing big initiatives or changes in the direction of the church. He casts vision with the men. He laughs with them. He pours into them spiritually. He tells them how vital they are to achieving goals, including and valuing them in the enterprise. He points men to the men's network meant to develop them into leaders. He appoints leaders and directs the men to follow their leadership. At the end of the meetings, the men pray for their pastor.

What do you think this pastor's tactics mean to the men?

A pastor in New England always waits at the back of the line at church mealtimes. The men of the church have now begun to do likewise, though often they will usher him to the front of their "pack."

How do you think these men feel about their pastor?

A pastor in Kazakhstan invites a men's leader to preach once a month while he sits on the front row, later offering verbal affirmation.

What does this model to the church?

What does your pastor do
to let you know that you are
important to him?

CORE TEAM MEETING

REVIEW

As you begin your time together this week, here are a few questions to help start your group discussion.

1. Describe a rogue men's class or ministry. How does the Enemy use this kind of dysfunction to hamper the church's mission?

2. List ways your pastor has encouraged you to be a God's man.

3. How has God challenged you this week to be more active in leading your church and community toward Christ? Think specifically about what you sense Him saying to you about your responsibility and how to carry that out.

▶ In this video teaching session, Kenny explains the importance of creating a vision for your men's ministry. Listen carefully as he challenges us to develop a strong mission and vision statement and encourages us to strongly align with the senior pastor. We'll unpack this together after the video.

Watch Video Session 3:

"MISSION, VISION, AND ALIGNMENT" (31:00)

• Churches often don't know what the _____ for men's ministry is.

• A good vision and mission statement motivates people _____.

• A good vision and mission statement _____ resources.

• The pastor's _____ is your _____.

• The men in your church want to be seen as _____ in the life of the church.

▌▌ Review your notes from the video teaching and answer the following questions together.

1. Kenny described how men often don't know the goal of men's ministry. What do you know about your church's goals for men?

2. Describe ways the men of your church honor your pastor. How does he honor them in return?

3. Kenny warns of disconnected men and the harm they can cause. In what ways have you seen this tendency play out?

FOLLOW KENNY
On Twitter: @Kenny_Luck
Facebook.com/KennyLuck

IF YOU MISSED THIS WEEK'S VIDEO VISIT **LIFEWAY.COM/SLEEPINGGIANT** TO CATCH UP.

CORE TEAM ACTIVITY

Magic Wand, Part 1

Break into small groups and discuss this question together: If you had a magic wand and could "zap" the men's culture in your church, what would happen? (Below are some prompts to help. See also the chart on p. 55.)

1. What new behaviors would emerge?

2. How would relationships change?

3. What would men's spiritual lives look like?

4. How would the men see themselves in the context of church?

5. How would the community be impacted?

6. How would the men's church involvement change?

7. What would the men's culture feel like?

8. What kind of man would it attract?

9. How would it benefit new men in your church?

10. What results would be non-negotiable?

11. How would it impact the other ministries of the church?

12. How would your church's health be affected?

Whatever you build for your men going forward must accomplish those things in their lives.

Using the ideas generated above, write down some thoughts for a targeted mission and vision statement. Be prepared to discuss them during next week's activity.

CORE TEAM BIBLE STUDY

On the next few pages, you will find Scriptures to read and questions to discuss that will help your Core Team further develop an effective biblical philosophy for a movement of God's men. Read the Scripture and discuss together.

> *"The LORD answered me:*
> *Write down this vision;*
> *clearly inscribe it on tablets*
> *so one may easily read it.*
> *For the vision is yet for the appointed time;*
> *it testifies about the end and will not lie.*
> *Though it delays, wait for it,*
> *since it will certainly come and not be late." Habakkuk 2:2-3*

1. Why does the Lord tell Habakkuk to write the vision down? What is the importance of having a written vision statement for your men's ministry?

Receiving a vision from God should be important to us. A vision based on God's principles will be sure to flourish in His time. Your Core Team will want to return to that strong vision statement often.

"Trust in the L ORD *with all your heart,*
and do not rely on your own understanding;
think about Him in all your ways,
and He will guide you on the right paths." Proverbs 3:5-6

2. In what ways can we ensure that we don't rely on our own under-standing as we consider the pathway to effective men's ministry? What do you think negatively influences us?

While there are plenty of models for how to mobilize men and maxi-mize their strength, many of them draw more from culture than from Christ. As we develop the vision for our church's men's ministry, it is important to look to God and His Word for understanding.

"This is what the L ORD *of Hosts says: 'Do not listen to the*
words of the prophets who prophesy to you. They are making
you worthless. They speak visions from their own minds, not
from the L ORD *'s mouth.'" Jeremiah 23:16*

3. In what ways have our worldly efforts at reaching men been worthless? What is the evidence of a worthwhile men's ministry?

"You once spoke in a vision to Your loyal ones and said: 'I
have granted help to a warrior; I have exalted one chosen
from the people.'" Psalm 89:19

4. How does God grant us help to implement His vision in our church and community? How might the exalted warrior reference in Psalm 89:19 exhort the men of your church?

God's men long to hear a call to action, a call to battle. They want to know that their mission is clear, compelling, and from God. Then they will step out in faith to follow.

> *"The doorkeeper opens it for him, and the sheep hear his voice. He calls his own sheep by name and leads them out. When he has brought all his own outside, he goes ahead of them. The sheep follow him because they recognize his voice. They will never follow a stranger; instead they will run away from him, because they don't recognize the voice of strangers."* John 10:3-5

5. What are some of the voices of strangers that often beckon men to follow? How can we encourage our men to ignore those voices?

> *"A thief comes only to steal and to kill and to destroy. I have come so that they may have life and have it in abundance. I am the good shepherd. The good shepherd lays down his life for the sheep. The hired man, since he is not the shepherd and doesn't own the sheep, leaves them and runs away when he sees a wolf coming. The wolf then snatches and scatters them. This happens because he is a hired man and doesn't care about the sheep."* John 10:10-13

6. The picture of God's people being snatched and scattered hits all too close to home. What does this passage say about the importance of following the Good Shepherd? About those who truly represent His interests? Contrast God's man with the hireling.

Our world has been shattered by the influence of cultural man and the hirelings who have led him astray. Pray that God will raise up a godly generation of men who truly live for Him. Affirm your pastor for being a good shepherd.

> *"The elders who are good leaders should be considered worthy of an ample honorarium, especially those who work hard at preaching and teaching."* 1 Timothy 5:17

7. The Bible emphasizes not only the importance of preaching and teaching but of giving honor to those who do. How might your men honor their pastor?

When a pastor is honored in his church and in turn honors the people, a healthy church body results.

"But you, man of God, run from these things, and pursue righteousness, godliness, faith, love, endurance, and gentleness. Fight the good fight for the faith; take hold of eternal life that you were called to and have made a good confession about in the presence of many witnesses." 1 Timothy 6:11-12

8. Men must be warned to flee from the bad and encouraged to run toward the good—toward God. Safety comes in numbers—how does the "presence of many witnesses" help a man fight the good fight?

Men were never intended to go to war alone. We fight best when we are in a company of men led by an able leader whose marching orders come from God.

WRAP

- You must identify key issues, challenges, and opportunities in order to reach and grow the men of your culture.
- Ownership is key to the success of the mission.
- Mission and vision statements must be executable and achievable, vibrantly lived out in the lives of the men.
- Tap the passion, energy, gifts, and abilities that already exist in your church's men and direct them toward the target.
- Mission and Vision (defined)

  Mission: What your ministry is about, how we get to the desired state, what we do. It reflects today.

  Vision: Why your ministry exists. What the ministry is to become. The big, God-sized picture. Reflects the future.
- Rogue men's ministries operate independently and are often disconnected from the overall mission and vision of the church.
- Developing men who guard the vision and serve others will create an explosive men's culture for Christ.
- Loyalty is built through relationship and service.
- Loyalty and submission to spiritual authority must replace dissension and division.

PRAY TOGETHER

NEXT WEEK

[ ] Read session introduction on page 75

[ ] Complete Work at Home study

[ ] Review enrichment options

[ ] Read *Sleeping Giant* chapters 11-12 (optional)

FOLLOW KENNY

On Twitter: @Kenny_Luck
Facebook.com/KennyLuck

STRONG FUNNELS AND PATHWAYS

On a warm afternoon in 2011, R.J. Epps was minding his own business when a loud roar like that of a locomotive suddenly filled his ears. As the reality of what was occurring settled into the 8-year-old's mind, he found himself drawn in and caught up by the 200-mph winds of one of the worst tornadoes ever to strike Alabama. R.J. was ripped from his home as the walls and roof collapsed and belongings scattered. Incredibly, little R.J. found himself landing gently just 30 feet from the home site and having only a few scrapes and bruises to testify to his adventure. The Epps family marveled over their miracle in the midst of great tragedy for the city of Tuscaloosa.[1]

A funnel cloud can be a powerful force indeed. Just as funnels have the power to draw men in destructively, they can also be powerful forces for good when applied creatively to men's ministry. These funnels can be understood in terms of powerful events, transforming Bible studies, and effective relationships rooted in biblical principles. As leaders discover the needs that most affect men, they can then build funnels or pathways to help them lock on to the church's vision and to get them on a spiritual pathway to success. Activities and topics that resonate with men outside your church pull them in for regular contact with God's Word, energizing them with hope as their greatest concerns in life are addressed and opportunities for blessing and growth follow.

> TO THOSE WHO ARE WITHOUT THAT LAW, [I BECAME] LIKE ONE WITHOUT THE LAW—NOT BEING WITHOUT GOD'S LAW BUT WITHIN CHRIST'S LAW—TO WIN THOSE WITHOUT THE LAW. TO THE WEAK I BECAME WEAK, IN ORDER TO WIN THE WEAK. I HAVE BECOME ALL THINGS TO ALL PEOPLE, SO THAT I MAY BY EVERY POSSIBLE MEANS SAVE SOME. NOW I DO ALL THIS BECAUSE OF THE GOSPEL, SO I MAY BECOME A PARTNER IN ITS BENEFITS.
>
> 1 CORINTHIANS 9:21-23

In this session, Core Team members will develop strong funnels and pathways for men's ministry.

1. Timothy W. Martin, et. al., "Tornadoes Leave a Trail of Devastation," *The Wall Street Journal* [online], April 29, 2011 [cited Jan. 2012]. Available from the Internet: *http://online.wsj.com.*

ON THE FOLLOWING PAGES, YOU WILL FIND SEVERAL PERSONAL STUDY SECTIONS TO READ AND CONSIDER BEFORE YOUR CORE TEAM MEETING. YOU ARE ALSO ENCOURAGED TO ANSWER THE QUESTIONS AND JOURNAL IN THE SPACE PROVIDED.

Step 3: Strong Funnels

STRONG FUNNELS THAT RESONATE WITH MEN				
Pain	**Purpose**	**People**	**Power**	**Play**
Marriage	Cause	Fraternity	Influence	Fun
Family	Battle	Team	Significance	Laughter
Character	Loyalty	Accountability	Greatness	Pleasure
Temptation	Transcendence	Acceptance	Leadership	Risk
Isolation	Justice	Affirmation	Position	Adventure

Funnels are those topics and events meant to draw uninvolved, disconnected men into your men's group.

Ever ask why men don't come to church-sponsored events for men? We did. And we kept asking, realizing the necessity of getting men connected to our life and leader development process. Over time we came face to face with the unpleasant reality that our "funnels" for reaching and connecting men were not strong enough. So out went the pancake breakfast funnel. Out went the Monday Night Football funnel. Out went the expensive men's retreat funnel.

In came the most unlikely but powerful funnel that changed our men's ministry: pain.

The truth that pain is a powerful vehicle for reaching men was there the whole time in our own lives and in the stories of those around us. You see, pain is that one tough reality of life that every man faces. Building a platform that made the core pains of men the starting point from which every man in our church could begin to heal and grow was central to the leader-development journey all God's men need to take. A major benefit to creating this culture of transparency in our church was that it began to attract men from the outside. The funnel drew the men, and they were empowered through the involvement of God in our men's ministry.

> *"For I was hungry and you gave Me something to eat; I was thirsty and you gave Me something to drink; I was a stranger and you took me in."* Matthew 25:35

1. Jesus reminds us of the importance of meeting men at the point of their pain. Hunger, thirst, and loneliness are just a start. What other felt needs could be used to draw men into transformation through your men's ministry?

2. What role did pain play in deepening your involvement with church and interest in the things of God? How did God use His church to help you or someone you know?

LESSONS FROM THE BIG SCREEN. Watch the movie *Fireproof* together or with your family. Consider how your men's ministry might be able to create a funnel based on the important felt need for marriage help.

No Pole Vaulting

"Go to Class 101."

The year was 1989 and those words flowed out of my pastor's mouth in response to an ambitious young missionary who had just asked, "What do you have for leaders?" I remember feeling pretty stupid afterward for assuming myself a leader and asking the pastor if I—an unknown guy and new attendee—could jump right into his leadership community. So, after picking my ego up off the floor, exiting the room, and returning to church the following weekend, I signed my wife and myself up for "Class 101: Membership."

I soon came to appreciate my pastor's intentionality as classes 201, 301, and 401 followed.

In hindsight, I find his tactic brilliant. What a comfort it must have been to my pastor to know that he had in place a safe and strong funnel whereby people could enter a development process that would ensure that the right teachings and disciplines would be embedded into his people.

I never forgot that experience. Later, when setting up the process for men at Saddleback, I wanted a similar funnel in place to help people get on board with the vision and mission of men's ministry within our church. I can't tell you how many times I have said to men of all backgrounds and levels of maturity who want to get involved: "Go to our Get Healthy classes, and then we'll talk."

"Do nothing out of rivalry or conceit, but in humility consider others as more important than yourselves. Everyone should look out not only for his own interests, but for the interests of others. Make your own attitude that of Christ Jesus, who, existing in the form of God, did not consider equality with God as something to be used for His own advantage. Instead He emptied Himself by assuming the form of a slave, taking on the likeness of men." Philippians 2:3-7

3. What role do you think humility plays in building a strong leader? How did Jesus model this important trait?

4. How have you negatively used something positive for your own interest, perhaps even in the church? According to the passage above, what do you think is the key to living as a true God's man instead?

READ FOR YOURSELF

The Mind of Christ by T. W. Hunt

The Love Dare by Stephen Kendrick and Alex Kendrick

Shattered Dreams by Larry Crabb

Step 4: Strong Spiritual Pathway

Men who travel down the funnel and into involvement with their men's groups usually pose this mental question: Now that you've got me, what are you going to do with me?

Since men are built for significance and intend to pursue mission, you must have a strong spiritual pathway for God's men or they will quickly burn out and fall back to the ground. Or they might find some lesser pursuit outside your ministry.

A strong pathway is the core process on which to hang your entire men's ministry. If you don't have one, you need one. If you do have one, it better be rock solid and resonate with the men it's meant to guide. The purpose of this step in the *Sleeping Giant* process is to eliminate inspiration without progression, which leads to frustration, disappointment, and disconnection. Consider the following graphic which shows the dynamics of a strong connective funnel experience and the intentional linking of that to a solid pathway:

The Missing "Linkage"		
Provide a Strong Funnel in Order to:		**Point to and Provide a Strong Pathway in Order to:**
Gain Connection	**Intentionally and**	Continue Connection
Tap Motivation	**Proactively**	Build On Motivation
Provide Inspiration	**Address Questions**	Cast Vision
Produce Activation	**Men Are Asking In Their Minds**	Divine Calling
Begin Transformation		Strong Progression
New or Unactivated Believer		Deployed Leader

"The path of the righteous is like the first gleam of dawn, shining brighter and brighter until midday." Proverbs 4:18

5. How does the picture painted in Proverbs 4:18 relate to the ministry model of moving men from a funnel to a pathway?

6. Describe someone you have seen take a path similar to the one described in the Scripture above. How does his life reflect Christ to his family, church, and community?

Spiritual Formation

Men are doers, which is both a strength and a weakness. Since we are the "point and shoot" gender for the most part, churches must take care not to base their men's ministries along a "Ready … Fire! … Aim" model. The goal is not to get men all fired up for God while failing to have a process for directing all that firepower toward the good of the church. Instead, we need to remedy this trigger-happy methodology of unintentional men's ministry with "Ready … Aim … Fire!" While it's good to want your men to be excited for Christ and to transform, it's far better to equip them with a simple action plan that tells what they must do to realize the goal of growing in Christlikeness and serving the Lord. As the Core Team, you are going to be responsible for keeping men on this continuum.

"Ready … Aim … Fire!" must replace "Ready … Fire! … Aim." That's why, in the *Sleeping Giant* model, you see the "Be" goals (of core purpose transformations) and the "Do" actions required for those goals to be achieved together. Those actions are reflected in these phrases:

1. **GET IN …** with other men who share your convictions
2. **GET HEALTHY …** relationally and morally as a man
3. **GET STRONG …** biblically and spiritually as a disciple
4. **GET GOING …** into your personal leadership expressions of ministry and mission

When we talk about our men's pathway these are the four simple concepts that explain to interested guys everything we are about, from the process to the end-game. The best thing about the *Sleeping Giant* model is this: not a lot of explanation is required. Men understand these concepts immediately.

"Be doers of the word and not hearers only, deceiving yourselves. Because if anyone is a hearer of the word and not a doer, he is like a man looking at his own face in a mirror. For he looks at himself, goes away, and immediately forgets what kind of man he was. But the one who looks intently into the perfect law of freedom and perseveres in it, and is not a forgetful hearer but one who does good works—this person will be blessed in what he does." James 1:22-25

7. List ways the church tends to focus more on hearing than doing—especially as it relates to men's ministry.

8. How do you, a Core Team member, plan to help wake the sleeping giants in your church?

// **TESTIMONY** // ORPHANED CHRIS

Chris rose out of his seat and walked onto the field. God was clearly extending Himself in a supernatural way to Chris, speaking to him personally, and calling him to a new life. The music began to play, and the speaker invited all those men who felt God speaking to them to "get up out of your seats right now, make your way forward to the stadium field, and say yes to God with your feet." He had never been so inspired, so hopeful, or so personally convinced that this decision to become a Christian would be the best decision of his life.

After walking onto the field and giving his life to Christ, Chris searched in his local church for a strong pathway to build on his motivation to be God's man. The funnel was gone, and he needed someone to give him a process to follow in order to continue on the pathway. But Chris searched in vain, discovering instead a hodgepodge of Bible studies, annual events, and discipleship books for men that provided him no sense of the larger vision. Frustrated, Chris turned away from the local church and went back to the one place that seemed to understand his need for clarity, excellence, structure, vision, and purpose: the world.

Chris had a journey typical of many men who get on fire for Jesus but have nowhere to go next. My inward and outward reaction to Chris as he shared his story was the same as it was to the numerous men who'd told me similar tales. I said, "I am so sorry; that should never be." I wondered how many men I'd led to Christ who felt so much promise at the start, only to have the joy of their salvation grow stale because their churches had no process ready to receive these newborn boys and help them mature into God's men. I reflected on how men's ministry in general was reproducing the same cycle of frustration in men who, after great spiritual inspiration, made little spiritual progress.

In what ways is Chris's experience similar to your own?

How can the body of Christ ensure that more men are not left orphaned?

CORE TEAM MEETING

REVIEW

As you begin your time together this week, here are a few questions to help start your group discussion.

1. Which contact points or funnels has God used in your life to draw you into the community of God's men?

2. How would you describe your church's DNA? What about your men's ministry? What components would you like to see added?

3. How has God challenged you this week to be more active in leading your church and community toward Christ? Think specifically about your role in helping define and communicate the mission and vision of your church's men's ministry.

In this video teaching session, Kenny reminds us of the importance of offering strong funnels to reach men and creating a strong pathway to keep their spiritual formation going. Listen carefully as he challenges us to develop an intentional men's ministry. We'll unpack this together after the video.

Watch Video Session 4:

"STRONG FUNNELS AND PATHWAYS" *(31:00)*

- Strong _____ call out to those urgent needs that men are facing.

- Men are masters of _____ and _____.

- The four steps on the spiritual pathway for men are "Get ____," "Get _____," "Get _____," and "Get _____."

- The goal of "Get Strong" is an aggressive spiritual expression of the _____ _____ and the _____ _____.

Review your notes from the video teaching and answer the following questions together.

1. Kenny talked about how many men's ministry events are not effective. What are some things your church has attempted that haven't worked out so well? Explain.

2. Describe a class offering or event that did seem effective in reaching men in your community. What do you think made the difference?

3. What percentage of your church's efforts in men's ministry is targeted toward the most committed men? How might you shift that focus?

FOLLOW KENNY
On Twitter: @Kenny_Luck
Facebook.com/KennyLuck

IF YOU MISSED THIS WEEK'S VIDEO VISIT **LIFEWAY.COM/SLEEPINGGIANT** TO CATCH UP.

CORE TEAM ACTIVITY

Magic Wand, Part 2

Read the vision and mission statements for Every Man Ministries below:

Our Vision: The vision of Every Man Ministries is to revolutionize men's ministry, to free men spiritually, and to empower spiritual health worldwide.

Our Mission: The mission of Every Man Ministries is to help men Get In, Get Healthy, Get Strong, and Get Going.

After a lot of prayer and consideration, these are the statements we felt the Lord would use to keep us focused on kingdom work. As you develop your own vision and mission statement, make sure that it:

1. defines what could be

2. motivates people internally

3. draws everyone forward

4. defines your core priorities

5. rallies resources

6. creates purpose

7. defines the process

8. provides common language

9. defines how you serve others

10. unites energy and expression toward concrete goals

Using ideas generated last week, try to come up with clear, powerful vision and mission statements. These statements should communicate what you feel your church's men's ministry owes the men you'll help.

VISION:

MISSION:

CORE TEAM BIBLE STUDY

On the next few pages, you will find Scriptures to read and questions to discuss that will help your Core Team further develop an effective biblical philosophy for a movement of God's men. Read the Scripture and discuss together.

> *"Jesus took up the question and said: 'A man was going down from Jerusalem to Jericho and fell into the hands of robbers. They stripped him, beat him up, and fled, leaving him half dead. A priest happened to be going down that road. When he saw him, he passed by on the other side. In the same way, a Levite, when he arrived at the place and saw him, passed by on the other side. But a Samaritan on his journey came up to him, and when he saw the man, he had compassion. He went over to him and bandaged his wounds, pouring on olive oil and wine. Then he put him on his own animal, brought him to an inn, and took care of him. The next day he took out two denarii, gave them to the innkeeper, and said, "Take care of him. When I come back I'll reimburse you for whatever extra you spend."'"* Luke 10:30-35

1. In what ways have we been like these religious leaders in our approach to men's ministry?

A church's plans and approaches to men's ministry may look good on the surface, but they can often miss the real needs of the men in their churches. That may be in part because the ministry's existing leaders fail to recognize their own needs.

> "No one has greater love than this, that someone would lay down his life for his friends." *John 15:13*

2. Loyalty is a key value in a man's life. Describe a time when you saw it on display. How can you better incorporate this characteristic into your approach to service and missions?

In addition to a sense of loyalty among the men in their church, men crave and need true brotherhood and fraternity, which are displayed in Christian fellowship.

> "Flee from youthful passions, and pursue righteousness, faith, love, and peace, along with those who call on the Lord from a pure heart." *2 Timothy 2:22*

3. How does 2 Timothy 2:22 relate to Christian brotherhood?

> "For those He foreknew He also predestined to be conformed to the image of His Son, so that He would be the firstborn among many brothers." *Romans 8:29*

4. What role do you think identity plays in the way men express themselves? How should the knowledge that Christ counts us as brothers change our perspective?

A man's identity determines his energy and expression. Identifying with Christ and becoming more like Him is what discipleship is all about. Effective pathways move men in the right direction—toward a more complete identity in Christ.

> *"We all, with unveiled faces, are looking as in a mirror at the glory of the Lord and are being transformed into the same image from glory to glory; this is from the Lord who is the Spirit." 2 Corinthians 3:18*

5. What does this transformation look like in your men's ministry? What do you think is the significance of having a mirror to see that transformation take place?

> *"The Son of Man did not come to be served, but to serve, and to give His life—a ransom for many." Matthew 20:28*

6. In what ways did Jesus model service? How can you do likewise?

A man's true strength is in his ability to say no to himself and yes to others.

> *"Then Jesus came near and said to them, 'All authority has been given to Me in heaven and on earth. Go, therefore, and make disciples of all nations, baptizing them in the name of the Father and of the Son and of the Holy Spirit, teaching them to observe everything I have commanded you. And remember, I am with you always, to the end of the age.'"*
> *Matthew 28:18-20*

7. Do you think most guys in your church see Matthew 28:18-20 as personal marching orders from Jesus? Explain.

A man talks to others about that thing which he is most excited about and which has most impacted him. Whether he is excited about cars or Christ, men are messengers of what they like or love. Men are unique in the ways they communicate Christ to the world around them.

> *"This saying is trustworthy: 'If anyone aspires to be an overseer, he desires a noble work.' An overseer, therefore, must be above reproach, the husband of one wife, self-controlled, sensible, respectable, hospitable, an able teacher, not addicted to wine, not a bully but gentle, not quarrelsome, not greedy—one who manages his own household competently, having his children under control with all dignity. (If anyone does not know how to manage his own household, how will he take care of God's church?)"* 1 Timothy 3:1-5

8. We see here a description of what Paul expected of would-be leaders in the church. What funnels and pathways is your church currently using to help your men grow in their leadership potential?

In a safe group context, men need to go after core health in their own character and relationships. This involves an open discussion of temptation and compromise (moral health), views of women and marriage (marital health), leadership within the home (family health), and how masculine friendship and accountability work (relational health). In seeking to develop men who can be leaders in our churches, true health in these core areas is the goal.

WRAP

- One must discover underlying, unresolved issues for your culture of men in order to capture their passions.
- The felt needs of men will initially attract them to a ministry born out of their need.
- Uncommitted men in the church may be a direct reflection of their leadership.
- The spark has already been placed within men through the Holy Spirit and our challenge is to ignite it.
- Inspiration is not enough for those on a new journey; a follow-up place for them to land is critical to engaging men.
- Intentional funnel events and experiences need to link to a solid pathway for the development of a man.
- The developmental pathway must be consistent with the culture or DNA of your church.
- Ultimately one must be concerned with the life transformation of each man; this is one of the measures of success.

PRAY TOGETHER

NEXT WEEK

[ ] Read session introduction on page 97

[ ] Complete Work at Home study

[ ] Review enrichment options

[ ] Read *Sleeping Giant* chapters 13-14 (optional)

FOLLOW KENNY
On Twitter: @Kenny_Luck
Facebook.com/KennyLuck

STRONG

RELATIONAL CORE AND

GROUPS

Tank warfare builds its defense around interlocking fields of fire. Commanders know that any gap can have deadly consequences. That's why, prior to each mission, leaders draw up a sketch and lay markers to illustrate how each platoon and tank will cover an area of terrain that is overlapped on the left and right by friendly defenders. When every involved soldier is highly motivated and well trained and defenses are interrelated, the enemy won't stand a chance of getting through a gap and wreaking havoc.

An awesome fighting force is a good picture for what we hope to see in our men's ministry. We need strong men who depend upon each other to stay strong. The key concept is this: a strong spiritual pathway gives cohesion, but a strong relational infrastructure drives everything forward. Possessing a heart to reach men is good, but the men within your ranks will need to have their hearts filled with ongoing relational capital if they are to achieve long-term spiritual success. The quality of the relationships among the men in your ministry, then, is the difference between success and failure. And as we leave the place of strategy to advance into the area of implementation, the men of your church will need to work together.

> IRON SHARPENS IRON, AND ONE MAN SHARPENS ANOTHER.
>
> PROVERBS 27:17

In this session, Core Team members will develop a strong relational core and strong groups so that they can maintain a healthy men's ministry.

ON THE FOLLOWING PAGES, YOU WILL FIND SEVERAL PERSONAL STUDY SECTIONS TO READ AND CONSIDER BEFORE YOUR CORE TEAM MEETING. YOU ARE ALSO ENCOURAGED TO ANSWER THE QUESTIONS AND JOURNAL IN THE SPACE PROVIDED.

Step 5: Strong Relational Core

Churches often fail to cover the gap of relational depth within their men's ministry because they have other priorities on their minds. Things like committees, events, meetings, and projects tend to take precedence over cultivating strong personal bonds, thus stealing energy and diverting attention from the ministry's true purpose. An uncomfortable reason lies behind this crippling issue: focusing on other priorities requires fewer emotional encounters and physical demands than relationship building. In other words, relationships are messy and we tend to allow that to scare us away from authentically relating to our men. Busyness replaces relationship.

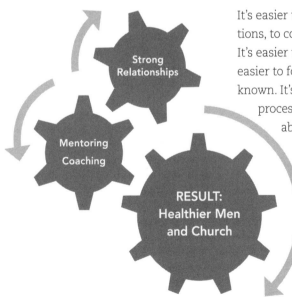

It's easier to answer Bible questions than to answer personal questions, to coordinate events for men rather than really get to know them. It's easier to advise a man biblically than to love a man biblically. It's easier to focus on what we know than to actually allow ourselves to be known. It's easier to talk about a process than to actually live out the process in community. It's easier to exercise authority and accountability than to extend affirmation and acceptance. It's easier to point someone to a book for a solution than to personally be the solution. It's easier to keep a safe distance than to be a safe harbor, to ask for men to step up for a mission than to step into their lives to minister. But here's the point: there is no such thing as strong but relationally shallow men's ministry.

"Jonathan then said to David, 'Go in the assurance the two of us pledged in the name of the LORD when we said: The LORD will be a witness between you and me and between my offspring and your offspring forever.' Then David left, and Jonathan went into the city." 1 Samuel 20:42

1. What role do you think Jonathan's friendship played in David's life, particularly in the toughest times? Explain.

2. How do you think that having the Lord witness their pledge of friendship contributed to their relationship? How might it have affected others?

LESSONS FROM THE BIG SCREEN. Watch a classic movie about friendship like *Brian's Song.* Consider the importance of committed friendship and its ability to give life and inspire hope.

Sticky Men

David and Jonathan shared a rare relationship that should be common in the family of God. At its center was an awareness that the sovereignty of God orchestrated their connection. Their mutual faith in Him energized their relationship as God's presence governed their interactions, even overseeing their accountability commitment to one another. That shared awareness, faith, energy, and commitment to accountability produced a bond that danger, depression, separation, isolation, and tribulation could not break. In fact, their bond illustrates the type of connection the *Sleeping Giant* process seeks to produce among the men in your church. As millions of men engage in divine connections, they will change the world for good and will empower the church.

> *"David was in the Wilderness of Ziph in Horesh when he saw that Saul had come out to take his life. Then Saul's son Jonathan came to David in Horesh and encouraged him in his faith in God, saying, 'Don't be afraid, for my father Saul will never lay a hand on you. You yourself will be king over Israel, and I'll be your second-in-command. Even my father Saul knows it is true.' Then the two of them made a covenant in the Lord's presence. Afterward, David remained in Horesh, while Jonathan went home."* 1 Samuel 23:15-18

3. Take each of the bulleted items in the sidebar related to a "sticky" men's culture and give an example of how your church does or could model this type of culture.

4. How do David and Jonathan reflect "sticky" men's culture? Explain.

"STICKY" MEN'S CULTURE EXHIBITS:

- true concern
- sacrifice
- spiritual support
- proactive encouragement
- a dedication to call out men's gifting
- an ability to speak prophetically into men's lives
- the seal of spiritual bonds
- a determination to refuel men for spiritual and emotional battles

Step 6: Strong Groups Concept

A huge sigh of relief always follows when I share with pastors that they will not have to change anything about their church's structure to make the *Sleeping Giant* men's ministry model happen. This is significant because all new initiatives need to be presented to pastors in such a way as to assure them that you aren't trying to create or add a new structure on top of what already exists. Smart pastors don't want to go to their members with another "ask"; don't want to do anything that might dilute church focus; and don't want to spend the precious relational capital they have accrued with congregants on something that does not drive the church's core vision forward.

The *Sleeping Giant* model can work in virtually all churches because almost all build their infrastructure around small-group concepts and dynamics: members already meet outside of the corporate gathering for worship, fellowship, and discipleship, whether in Sunday School or small groups in the home. The *Sleeping Giant* model seeks to take advantage of places where men gather, further drawing people who are already a part of the congregation into smaller units to advance relational connections and foster accelerated spiritual growth.

> *"Let us hold on to the confession of our hope without wavering, for He who promised is faithful. And let us be concerned about one another in order to promote love and good works, not staying away from our worship meetings, as some habitually do, but encouraging each other, and all the more as you see the day drawing near."* Hebrews 10:23-25

5. How do small groups help your church spur members toward "love and good works"? How do you think the *Sleeping Giant* model can help you be even more effective in this area?

6. In the Hebrews 10:23-25 passage, encouragement stands in contrast to avoiding meeting together. How have you been encouraged by church groups in the past? Plan to share an experience in your group time.

READ FOR YOURSELF

David: A Man of Passion and Destiny by Charles R. Swindoll

The Resolution for Men by Stephen Kendrick, Alex Kendrick, and Randy Alcorn

Small Groups with Purpose by Steve Gladen

A Place for Men

Men need a safe place to start connecting, a base from which they can begin tracking into your leadership development pathway. Many men's groups actually incubate inside of existing couples groups. The men there need to be intentionally activated, better connected with one another, and trained as future group leaders. Often they will intentionally subgroup outside of the normal group time, which is a healthy behavior. Connecting with other men on a small scale not only achieves the goal of spiritual health but also provides the structure a church needs to really care for the man. It allows a continuous and active connection point for new men reached by your ministry to enter into the funneling process of your church.

What will the end product look like? Men journey from the community to the crowd to the congregation to the committed to the core of church leadership. They come in through a men's funnel or the weekend funnel, get in a group, subgroup with men in that location, and start connecting and growing together. God's kingdom comes into that group of men, calls forth leaders from that group, and the church invites those men to experience the life and leader development pathway in a centralized and directed community of leaders on the church campus. The pathway is clear, strong, intentional, and rewarding. The pathway requires a commitment of time. The pathway is a combination of education and experiences. But by the end, God's man is healthy, strong, and going with velocity into His mission. The effort taken to realign your efforts with men now begins to pay for itself in church health, church growth, and church mobility.

> *"In the church that was at Antioch there were prophets and teachers: Barnabas, Simeon who was called Niger, Lucius the Cyrenian, Manaen, a close friend of Herod the tetrarch, and Saul. As they were ministering to the Lord and fasting, the Holy Spirit said, 'Set apart for Me Barnabas and Saul for the work I have called them to do.'"* Acts 13:1-2

7. Perhaps you remember when Saul (who would become Paul) was introduced into the group of believers. Now we see him referred to as a leader. What does this tell you about the church at Antioch?

8. What do we learn from Barnabas and Saul's commissioning?

MEN'S NETWORK

Senior Pastor
Men's Pastor
Men's Leaders
Men's Groups
Men of the Church
Men in the Community

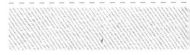

// **TESTIMONY** // KENNY, A SURVIVOR

I survived my own family's struggle with alcoholism. I survived being left alone to fight through the minefields of my childhood, adolescent, and teen years. I survived economically, socially, relationally, and spiritually; I endured loneliness, rejection, and abuse. Miraculously and by God's grace, I even survived the lure and bondage of addiction. I survived the slimy pits of fatherlessness and a broken quest for sonship— long keeping all of these things to myself, never recognizing their toll on me, my relationships, and my ministry. I survived the sicknesses of character these secrets unleashed in my life as my conduct disconnected me from God and people.

So why punish you with my past? To illustrate how my old patterns of thinking and living as a survivor dramatically impacted my ability to connect authentically with people as a man, as a husband, as a men's pastor, and as a leader. For men in general, and for me, in particular, this relationship stuff is hard.

Survivors have to be loved back to health.

In what ways have you been a survivor?

How have you been or need to be loved back to health?

CORE TEAM MEETING

REVIEW

As you begin your time together this week, here are a few questions to help start your group discussion.

1. How does the culture of your church compare to the "sticky" men's culture illustrated by David and Jonathan's relationship?

2. In what ways have small groups of men helped you in your journey as a God's man?

3. How has God challenged you this week to be more active in leading your church and community toward Christ? Think specifically about the developmental pathway you as a Core Leadership Team are putting into place to connect the men in your church in a meaningful way.

In this video teaching session, Kenny reminds us of the importance of building a strong relational core with men and relying on strong groups to help maximize the effectiveness of our churches. Listen carefully as he challenges us to continue waking the Sleeping Giant. We'll unpack this together after the video.

Watch Video Session 5:

"STRONG RELATIONAL CORE AND GROUPS" (33:00)

- A strong relationship _____ drives an effective men's ministry and gives it meaning.

- There is no such thing as a strong but relationally _____ men's ministry.

- Authentic relational _____ bring powerful relational _____ that you can spend on strategic "asks."

- A strong relational dynamic in the men's ministry starts with the _____ and _____ _____.

- The church must have one _____ to the men and one place for them to start the _____.

FOLLOW KENNY

On Twitter: @Kenny_Luck
Facebook.com/KennyLuck

Review your notes from the video teaching and answer the following questions together.

1. **Why do you think Kenny says the quality of relationships among the men in your ministry is the gap between success and failure?**

2. **Describe a time when you felt unconnected in a crowd. How did it affect you? Explain.**

3. **How much time does your church ask from the men in a given week or month? How can you help God's men steward this precious resource?**

IF YOU MISSED THIS WEEK'S VIDEO VISIT **LIFEWAY.COM/SLEEPINGGIANT** TO CATCH UP.

CORE TEAM ACTIVITY

Problems That Groups Solve

Read these benefits of subgrouping, then discuss how your church might profit in similar ways. Remember, you don't have to change your structure to use the *Sleeping Giant* model, so some of these may not apply in your context:

1. Subgrouping eliminates the need to have pure men's groups as a core strategy. If a man is married we tell him to join a couples group or a family group because we know he will be encouraged to connect with the men of that group on a regular basis.

2. Subgrouping eliminates the unhealthy dynamic of men keeping secrets. We intentionally gather the men within these social networks so that they can address issues they are reluctant to mention in the presence of women.

3. Subgrouping allows men to be in community with each other and remain in proximity to the spouses and children within the larger group. This provides for meaningful transparency and accountability.

4. Subgrouping allows the women to grow familiar with the men, wives, and life stories of those within their husbands' men's group. This helps them be more supportive of the connection versus suspicious.

5. Time—the most precious commodity a man has—is conserved by only having to commit to one set of relationships and friendships versus two sets. The man has a life group and men's group in one. The wife's needs are met, the man's needs are met, the couple's needs are met, and their children are exposed to spiritual community.

6. Subgrouping helps the church escape the "silo" effect, avoiding competition for people's time and allowing them to start cooperating for the health of all involved.

7. Church health, group health, and individual health of members is accelerated dramatically.

CORE TEAM BIBLE STUDY

On the next few pages, you will find Scriptures to read and questions to discuss that will help your Core Team further develop an effective biblical philosophy for a movement of God's men. Read the Scripture and discuss together.

> *"The Word became flesh and took up residence among us. We observed His glory, the glory as the One and Only Son from the Father, full of grace and truth."* John 1:14

1. How did Jesus demonstrate both grace and truth throughout His ministry? In what ways can these two concepts serve as anchors for men's ministry?

Many churches are adept at providing truth to men but are too slow to apply grace, the very thing that men most need to heal. These are the two character qualities that the God-man wants men to experience personally before reproducing in the lives of other men.

"I searched for a man among them who would repair the wall and stand in the gap before Me on behalf of the land so that I might not destroy it, but I found no one." Ezekiel 22:30

2. Why do you think so many spiritual gaps exist in the land? What can we do to ensure that there are God's men prepared to cover those gaps?

Men are able to get healthy in groups that are committed to holding fast to truth while applying much-needed grace. They are then able to mind the gaps created by cultural decline as they get strong together.

"Every day they devoted themselves to meeting together in the temple complex, and broke bread from house to house. They ate their food with a joyful and humble attitude, praising God and having favor with all the people. And every day the Lord added to them those who were being saved."
Acts 2:46-47

3. In Acts 2:46-47, circle the actions men take together. Describe the pattern that develops.

"Then he went on to Derbe and Lystra, where there was a disciple named Timothy, the son of a believing Jewish woman, but his father was a Greek. The brothers at Lystra and Iconium spoke highly of him. Paul wanted Timothy to go with him, so he took him and circumcised him because of the Jews who were in those places, since they all knew that his father was a Greek. As they traveled through the towns, they delivered the decisions reached by the apostles and elders at Jerusalem for them to observe. So the churches were strengthened in the faith and increased in number daily."
Acts 16:1-5

4. What leadership principles do you see in this passage as these groups of men did life together? How did the church benefit?

Groups of God's men were forming ranks and leaders were being raised up among them to the benefit of the church and the communities around them. We see not only spiritual growth but also numerical growth once God's men were mobilized.

"Brothers, if someone is caught in any wrongdoing, you who are spiritual should restore such a person with a gentle spirit, watching out for yourselves so you also won't be tempted. Carry one another's burdens; in this way you will fulfill the law of Christ. For if anyone considers himself to be something when he is nothing, he deceives himself." Galatians 6:1-3

5. What healthy character traits does Paul describe in Galatians 6:1-3?

"Two are better than one because they have a good reward for their efforts. For if either falls, his companion can lift him up; but pity the one who falls without another to lift him up." Ecclesiastes 4:9-10

6. Describe a situation in which a man without a support system fell. What does Ecclesiastes 4:9-10 tell us about the importance of surrounding ourselves with other God's men?

Maximum church health is achieved when the weekend structure is connected meaningfully to a small-group structure aligned strategically for the sake of men. Core Team, we and the men of the church need each other if we are to be successful God's men.

"Confess your sins to one another and pray for one another, so that you may be healed. The urgent request of a righteous person is very powerful in its effect." James 5:16

7. What kind of healing needs to take place in your life and in the lives of the men around you? What role do you think prayer will play in that healing? How can groups help?

"Praise the God and Father of our Lord Jesus Christ, the Father of mercies and the God of all comfort. He comforts us in all our affliction, so that we may be able to comfort those who are in any kind of affliction, through the comfort we ourselves receive from God." 2 Corinthians 1:3-4

8. Circle the word comfort every time it appears in this passage. What is the relationship between God's role as Comforter and ours in our families, churches, and communities? What do we learn from this verse about healing and comfort?

Men's ministry is best delivered in the context of small-group dynamics or a modified model that advances masculine connection where encouragement, prayer, and accountability can happen. Groups can be centers of healing for men.

WRAP

- The more relational capital you have with your leadership, the more spiritual authority you have in men's lives.
- The more relational capital your leaders have with the men coming into your process, the more spiritual authority they have with those men to bring them through the process and into leadership.
- The more relational capital you have flowing among your men, the faster they will respond to initiatives and needs in the church.
- Your men's ministry must drive the core vision and structure of your church forward.
- Leaders must be the first to adopt and demonstrate behaviorally the spiritual mission that you wish to teach tactically.
- The intentional developmental pathway encompasses a mixture of exposing men to education, providing growth experiences for them, and helping them find a place to express their gifts and abilities.

PRAY TOGETHER

NEXT WEEK

[ ] Read session introduction on page 119

[ ] Complete Work at Home study

[ ] Review enrichment options

[ ] Read *Sleeping Giant* chapters 15-16 (optional)

FOLLOW KENNY

On Twitter: @Kenny_Luck
Facebook.com/KennyLuck

"GO" TIME

A Michigan pastor wants to do everything he can to reach out to people who feel cut off from God. He decides to open a tattoo parlor at his church, building on his belief that mainstream religion is ineffective and irrelevant to many people in his community. By setting traditions aside, he is able to use tattoo art to share the good news and to reach people where they are.

On the other side of the world, a young Chinese pastor with little education moves to a war-torn Muslim village so that he can share the gospel there. Hoping to build an inroad into the community, he opens a restaurant and learns a whole new way of cooking so as not to offend. He has to leave behind his favorite recipes since most of them involve pork. Not only has he found opportunities to share Christ in his new situation, but he's gotten good at cooking lamb.

TO THE WEAK I BECAME WEAK, IN ORDER TO WIN THE WEAK. I HAVE BECOME ALL THINGS TO ALL PEOPLE, SO THAT I MAY BY EVERY POSSIBLE MEANS SAVE SOME.

1 CORINTHIANS 9:22

If we want our men's ministry efforts to be successful, we must learn from men like these. We've got to meet the men in our communities where they are and then develop a system for moving them to where they need to be. Helping men Get In, Get Healthy, Get Strong, and then Get Going to reach other men for Christ is what men's ministry is all about.

In this session, Core Team members will plan and implement the *Sleeping Giant* strategy for men's ministry.

This is a pretty heavy work session at the close of the Core Team experience, so roll up your sleeves. It's "Go" Time!

ON THE FOLLOWING PAGES, YOU WILL FIND SEVERAL PERSONAL STUDY SECTIONS TO READ AND CONSIDER BEFORE YOUR CORE TEAM MEETING. YOU ARE ALSO ENCOURAGED TO ANSWER THE QUESTIONS AND JOURNAL IN THE SPACE PROVIDED.

Functional Dynamics

The three phases shown in the following charts demonstrate just how to move men already engaged in men's ministry through the remaining stages of the *Sleeping Giant* process.

These three phases are the functional dynamics of Get In, Get Healthy, Get Strong, and Get Going and provide meaning and context for *Sleeping Giant*'s philosophical architecture. This is what the ministry should look like, feel like, sound like, and live like as it practically projects and reflects biblical principles. It is the intuitive process and the theological application of quality men's ministry. These are the results we are watching for and demanding out of our leaders at each phase. This is what we model by example and message between the lines.

> *"As you have received Christ Jesus the Lord, walk in Him, rooted and built up in Him and established in the faith, just as you were taught, overflowing with gratitude. Be careful that no one takes you captive through philosophy and empty deceit based on human tradition, based on the elemental forces of the world, and not based on Christ."* Colossians 2:6-8

LESSONS FROM THE BIG SCREEN. Watch *We Bought a Zoo* to see how one man decided on a vision and found healing as he followed it. Consider the *Sleeping Giant* principles that apply.

1. This passage says Christians should be rooted, built up, established. How do you think the *Sleeping Giant* phases help to accomplish that?

2. What are the dangers associated with not helping men become grounded through healthy men's ministry?

Phase 1: Proactively Defining and Meeting Needs

Felt Needs of Men	Principles	Biblical Values
Purpose	Touch need/pain	"Hungry?" Feed.
Marital Health	Transform his life	"Naked?" Clothe.
Sexual Integrity	Take down the pathway	Matthew 25:35
Family Health		
Authentic Friendships		
Significance		
Character Growth		

Outcomes Sought	Tools Used Here
Connects to other men	Get Healthy Curriculum/DVDs
Connects to men's ministry	"Intimacy"
Feels helped	"Temptation"
The spiritual pathway is explained	"Family"
Goes to the next core health class	"Friendship"
Character issues addressed	

Vision Cast

1 Timothy 3 Leader Requirements Met

Being tracked relationally through the pathway

Key Result

The helped and transformed man wants to know: "What's next?"

Duration

32 Weeks

Phase 2: Discipling for Depth

Leader Needs	Principles	Biblical Values
Spiritual Formation	Integrity of heart	Luke 6:40
Spiritual Disciplines	Integration of life	Colossians 1:28–29
Leadership Training	Involvement in experiences	Colossians 2:6–8
Biblical Worldview		
Leadership Experiences		
Gifting Identified		
Call to Ministry		

Outcomes Sought	Tools Used Here
Leader is selected	Get Strong Curriculum/DVDs
Leader is called	Risk (faith)
Leader is being trained	Dream (Christlikeness)
Leader is being mentored	Fight (spiritual warfare)
Leading a small group	Soar (Holy Spirit)
Joining leadership community	Foundations

Key Result

The helped and transformed man wants to know: "What's next?"

Duration

32 Weeks

Phase 3: Deploy to Lead

Assignment Needs	Principles	Biblical Values
Church small group leader	Responsible for men	2 Timothy 2:2
Get Healthy class facilitator	Reproducing leaders	Matthew 28:18–20
Men's Ministry Leader	Replacing Staff	Romans 15:20
Church Ministry Leader		Ephesians 2:10
High School Leader		
Kids Ministry Leader		
Missions Team Leader		
Men's Pastor in Another Church		

Outcomes Sought	Tools Used Here
In a men's group	Leadership Books
Leading a men's group	Devotional Books
Part of Leadership Community	Training Seminars
Recruiting New Leaders	Spiritual growth tools
Teaching Pathway	Leadership Assessment tools
Training Others	
Cross Trained	
Spiritual Health Plan	
Continuing Education	

Key Result

The reproducing leader asks, "Who else can I bring along the journey?"

Duration

Lifetime

Equipping Leaders

Equipping leaders begins as each man is funneled into the process. As soon as possible, you'll need to get every man plugged into a small group. Once there, he'll experience the church defining and meeting his deepest felt needs as a man, calling him into a discipleship relationship and process, and commissioning him to serve the body and share Christ with others. In this way, the guy who visits a home barbecue or church one day goes from being "every man" to being an equipped leader on mission for God.

> "He personally gave some to be apostles, some prophets, some evangelists, some pastors and teachers, for the training of the saints in the work of ministry, to build up the body of Christ, until we all reach unity in the faith and in the knowledge of God's Son, growing into a mature man with a stature measured by Christ's fullness." Ephesians 4:11-13

3. God intended for the church to grow an abundance of leaders for the work that needs to be done. How does the *Sleeping Giant* process help men attain this maturity and stature?

4. Think of a lay leader you know in your church. How is he currently serving? How does his story illustrate principles of leadership development?

Where Are You?

During your Core Team time this week, you'll have the opportunity to respond to the revelations you've received regarding men's ministry. As you close your Work at Home time, fill out the included assessment and consider the principles you've learned. Spend this session seeking God's path for implementation in your church.

- **Reflect honestly.** The questions are designed to provide a starting point for your church and a no-nonsense basis for your action plan.

- **Recognize reality.** There are no good or bad or right or wrong answers on the assessment. There is only truth and reality. That's the best place to begin the process. For example, those whose churches have little to nothing happening will stop scoring points after the first few questions. Others will score on most. It is only essential that the score reflect reality. You can't change what you don't acknowledge.

- **Respond practically.** Near the end of this session, we will suggest specific pathways of action for you to consider based on your score.

Pray for your pastor and Core Team as you prepare for this week's Core Team time. The men in your church and community need you focused and spirit-filled if you are to rouse the Sleeping Giant.

"If the ax is dull, and one does not sharpen its edge, then one must exert more strength; however, the advantage of wisdom is that it brings success." Ecclesiastes 10:10

5. In what ways might a men's ministry "dull" over time? How does your Core Team working together mean that less strength is exerted for greater effect?

6. Consider the magic wand question discussed previously (p. 65). How has your idea of what successful men's ministry looks like changed since the beginning of the study? Explain.

READ FOR YOURSELF

Spiritual Leadership by Henry Blackaby and Richard Blackaby

Jesus on Leadership by C. Gene Wilkes

Transformational Church by Thom Rainer and Ed Stetzer

Sleeping Giant Assessment, Part 1

Fill out the assessment by circling your answers. When you gather with the Core Team, you will have an opportunity to compare results and create a consensus on where your church stands.

1. Our church clearly understands the unresolved issues our men face.

a. Untrue	0
b. Mostly untrue	1
c. Neutral	2
d. Mostly true	3
e. True	4

2. Our church prioritizes impact and acts on key issues facing our men.

a. Untrue	0
b. Mostly untrue	1
c. Neutral	2
d. Mostly true	3
e. True	4

3. Our church provides experiences that involve the men and links them to an intentional developmental process.

a. Untrue	0
b. Mostly untrue	1
c. Neutral	2
d. Mostly true	3
e. True	4

MAKE SURE THAT YOU COMPLETE THIS ASSESSMENT BEFORE YOUR CORE TEAM TIME.

4. Our church communicates in ways that resonate with men and causes them to activate or connect with the church, i.e., men become men in the company of other men.

a. Untrue	0
b. Mostly untrue	1
c. Neutral	2
d. Mostly true	3
e. True	4

5. Our church has a regularly scheduled men's breakfast or meeting.

a. Never	0
b. Weekly	4
c. Quarterly	3
d. Bi-Yearly	2
e. Annually	1

6. Our men's breakfast or meeting intentionally connects men to small groups.

a. Untrue	0
b. Mostly untrue	1
c. Neutral	2
d. Mostly true	3
e. True	4

7. Our men's breakfast or meeting has teaching that changes men's lives for the better.

a. Untrue	0
b. Mostly untrue	1
c. Neutral	2
d. Mostly true	3
e. True	4

8. There is evidence that men have connected as a result of our men's breakfast or meeting.

    a. Untrue   0
    b. Mostly untrue   1
    c. Neutral   2
    d. Mostly true   3
    e. True   4

9. Men are engaging in weekly Bible studies and other men's offerings.

    a. Untrue   0
    b. Mostly untrue   1
    c. Neutral   2
    d. Mostly true   3
    e. True   4

10. Our church provides topical classes that address the needs of men.

    a. Untrue   0
    b. Mostly untrue   1
    c. Neutral   2
    d. Mostly true   3
    e. True   4

11. Our events, classes, and Bible studies for men connect men to small groups.

    a. Untrue   0
    b. Mostly untrue   1
    c. Neutral   2
    d. Mostly true   3
    e. True   4

12. We have established direction, purpose, and goals (mission and/or vision) for our men's ministry.

    a. Untrue   0
    b. Mostly untrue   1
    c. Neutral   2
    d. Mostly true   3
    e. True   4

13. The men's direction, purpose, and goals (mission and/or vision) are consistent with our churches mission and vision.

    a. Untrue   0
    b. Mostly untrue   1
    c. Neutral   2
    d. Mostly true   3
    e. True   4

14. The direction, purpose, and goals (mission and/or vision) of the men's ministry can be stated by the men of the ministry.

    a. Untrue   0
    b. Mostly untrue   1
    c. Neutral   2
    d. Mostly true   3
    e. True   4

15. We have a documented and communicated developmental pathway that our men can and have shared with others.

    a. Untrue   0
    b. Mostly untrue   1
    c. Neutral   2
    d. Mostly true   3
    e. True   4

16. Our church has an effective leader development process for men that results in men actively serving in the church.

a. Untrue	0
b. Mostly untrue	1
c. Neutral	2
d. Mostly true	3
e. True	4

17. Our men's leaders are constantly raising new leaders.

a. Untrue	0
b. Mostly untrue	1
c. Neutral	2
d. Mostly true	3
e. True	4

18. The majority of our groups are facilitated/taught by:

a. Pastors	1
b. Deacons or Elders	2
c. Volunteers	3
d. All of the above	4

19. Our developmental pathway for men is known and can be/has been communicated to others by our men.

a. Untrue	0
b. Mostly untrue	1
c. Neutral	2
d. Mostly true	3
e. True	4

20. Our developmental pathway is well known to the men and is aligned with the values and processes of our church.

a. Untrue	0
b. Mostly untrue	1
c. Neutral	2
d. Mostly true	3
e. True	4

DEMOGRAPHICS ONLY - UNSCORED

21. Our church has regularly scheduled: (circle all that apply)

    a. Participation sports (basketball, golf, softball)
    b. Annual retreats or conferences
    c. Quarterly meetings/rallies
    d. Topical seminars on things like finances or home leadership
    e. Spectator sporting events
    f. Weekly Bible study
    g. Other events not listed above

22. Our church has: (circle all that apply)

    a. Weekend services
    b. Midweek services
    c. Sunday School
    d. Small groups
    e. Men's small groups

// **TESTIMONY** // GAP MEN

"I tell you what I want, and what I have on my heart. I believe we have got to have gap-men to stand between the laity and the ministers. ... Take men that have the gifts and train them for the work of reaching the people." —D.L. Moody

Ben was a typical college student—at least a typical married college student. He and Linda married just a year after arriving at school. Sadly, both of them came into the relationship with huge holes in their hearts—holes that they each hoped the other could fill. Only a few months into their marriage, Ben knew that Linda couldn't heal his.

Ben took a job at a local cafeteria where a godly young man, Frank, worked as a supervisor. Frank, having given his heart to Christ a few years before, had decided to be a gap man much like the late evangelist D.L. Moody desired to see. Frank missed no opportunity to share his faith. He also made sure that he modeled his faith, so much so that it sometimes made Ben uncomfortable.

Ben thought Frank was a nut job; but when things got even worse with his marriage, it was Frank he turned to. There was something different about Frank, and Ben knew instinctively he could help.

Frank invited Ben to play basketball at his church with a group of men. Ben felt at ease hanging out with the guys, and he realized just how much he missed a sense of fraternity. These guys were different than any he'd hung out with before. They were real. And while they were fierce competitors on the court, they were honoring of one another and their wives who sometimes came up in conversation. These men had been changed by Jesus Christ and were committed to standing in the gap for Him. On the way home Ben decided that he too wanted to be a gap man. He gave his heart—and his marriage—to Christ.

How can you stand in the cultural gaps that exist?

What can you do to help another man cross the gap and find a sense of belonging?

CORE TEAM MEETING

REVIEW

As you begin your time together this week, here are a few questions to help start your group discussion.

1. Think of your community and imagine it completely void of men willing to stand up for right. To which movie or novel might you compare it? What will you do to save it?

2. Describe the type of leader you hope your men will be three years after joining your men's ministry.

3. How has God challenged you this week to be more active in leading your church and community toward Christ? Think specifically about how authentic your relationships are with other men in your ministry.

▶ In this video teaching session, Kenny reminds us of the importance of understanding ministry context and guides us in the next steps to successfully awakening the Sleeping Giant. We'll unpack this together after the video.

Watch Video Session 6:

"'GO' TIME" (28:00)

• Your men's ministry must have the _____ and _____ to meet any man that encounters it with meaning and in context.

• The *Sleeping Giant* process makes every man a _____ and invites him into the _____ of believers.

• The men have to know that your _____ and your _____ are rock solid.

⏸ Review your notes from the video teaching and answer the following questions together.

1. What do you think led to Steve going to church and being open to what Bill had to say? How might that affect our outlook on "church time"?

2. With whom have you seen a similar experience or transition at your church? Which processes allowed for change to occur?

3. Before comparing notes on your *Sleeping Giant* assessments, which scenario do you think best applies to your church?

FOLLOW KENNY
On Twitter: @Kenny_Luck
Facebook.com/KennyLuck

IF YOU MISSED THIS WEEK'S VIDEO VISIT **LIFEWAY.COM/SLEEPINGGIANT** TO CATCH UP.

CORE TEAM ACTIVITY

Sleeping Giant Assessment, Part 2

Determine Context

Time to determine your context. Take some time to gather information and resources to develop your specific *Sleeping Giant* process. Place an "X" by each segment you already have. This will help you to see quantitatively where you currently stand.

__ Pancake Breakfast (or other entry event)

__ Other Events

__ Topical Classes (short-term)

__ Ongoing Bible Studies

__ Groups

__ Pathway

__ Leader Pathway

__ Reproducing Leaders/Pipeline

__ Servant Teachers/Facilitators

__ Vision

Now let's compare scores from the *Sleeping Giant* Assessment that you completed during your Work at Home time and arrive at a consensus on where you are as a church. Once you have a good feel for which scenario best applies to your context, take out a calendar and begin planning your next year of awesome, reproductive, and challenging men's ministry. Our prayer is that the Sleeping Giant in your church will indeed be awakened!

SCORE: 0 - 16 // SCENARIO #1

Description: No or infrequent meetings and/or connection places, no strategy or plans for men.

Action Plan:
- Meet with the pastor to understand his mission and vision for your church.
- Conduct a Magic Wand meeting with the pastor and men's ministry leaders or potential leaders to determine your desired outcomes.
- Identify funnel events that can help gather men.

SCORE: 17 - 28 // SCENARIO #2

Description: Breakfasts, events, and classes, but no vision implemented, no leader development, no pathway.

Action Plan:
- Implant vision and mission (start using the language of your vision) to your men as part of your event.
- Use the funnel event to connect men to one another (sit at tables).
- Use discussion questions and talk time to get guys used to interacting with one another about significant matters.

SCORE: 29 - 37 // SCENARIO #3

Description: Programs (Bible studies), events, and classes, but no groups, no leader development, no pathway, no vision implemented.

Action Plan:

- Gather rosters from funnel events and challenge men to meet again outside of the event.
- Seek out known group leaders or those you believe could lead a group of guys to connect from funnel events.
- Create an intentional developmental pathway with your existing leadership.
- Develop a formal funnel strategy to move men from attendance to connection.
- Develop a leader selection plan to use with the men who are currently moving through the process. These are your future leaders.

SCORE: 38 - 66 // SCENARIO #4

Description: Programs (Bible studies), events, classes, and groups, but no pathway, no vision implemented, no leader development.

Action Plan:

- Share an intentional development pathway for the men who attend.
- Share the vision and mission each and every time they meet.
- Challenge men to take initial steps now in their spiritual growth and plant the seed that will lead to leader development as they move from Get Healthy to Get Strong.
- Host a *Sleeping Giant* training event.
- Begin forming a relational support structure to support forming groups from pastor to coaches/mentors to group leaders.
- Start to develop facilitators for additional men's small group, on-campus studies. Share facilitation.
- Challenge every leader to bring along men who are taking their next leadership step. Mentor those identified as potential leaders.

SCORE: 67 + // SCENARIO #5

Description: Programs (Bible studies), events, classes, groups, pathway aligned with values and process for leader development, reproducing leaders, vision—full integration.

Action Plan:

- The challenge for you will be consistency of culture, encouragement of leadership, and creative ways to get more men into the funnel. Continue to run connection events to keep filling and launching new groups.
- Consider having Kenny come to your church and conduct a conference. He will support your process and activate the new men you invite to get connected to your pathway. He has personally connected tens of thousands of men into a life and leader development process.
- Look at the Get Healthy and Get Strong tools connected to the *Sleeping Giant* pathway to stay current and fresh in your men's ministry process.

STAYING CONNECTED Tell us what works for you! Share stories with us and ask questions. Join the network of churches that are using *Sleeping Giant*. We want to hear from you!

Kenny Luck
For speaking or conferences:
kennylu@saddleback.com

Tom Crick
For *Sleeping Giant* training:
tomc@saddleback.com

WRAP

- You must find the men in your church who are willing to pay the time tax to enter other men's lives in a meaningful way.
- Identify and engage what God has already placed in men's hearts.
- A man's pain is a doorway to be able to minister to him and is often the impetus for him seeking help.
- A man who has walked a similar path is ideal to reach other hurting men. He can help bring meaning and context and knows the process.
- Your men's ministry must have a structure that meets needs and bridges men into leadership and meaningful ministry.
- PHASING
  Phase 1: Proactively define and meet needs.
  Phase 2: Disciple for depth.
  Phase 3: Deploy to lead.

The process is successful when core leaders can walk away and the ministry continues to reproduce.

PRAY TOGETHER

Congratulations! Your Core Team is on the pathway to Get In, Get Healthy, Get Strong, and Get Going. Soon the men of your church will follow. May the Lord bless you as you begin your first Get Healthy study in the coming weeks.

FOLLOW KENNY
On Twitter: @Kenny_Luck
Facebook.com/KennyLuck

LEADER NOTES
MESSAGE TO THE PASTOR

First, view the message to the pastor on the DVD to hear Kenny's heart and to familiarize yourself with the *Sleeping Giant* message. Be sure to get *Sleeping Giant* Core Team Workbooks to your Core Team members prior to the first session so they can complete the Work at Home section before your first group meeting. You may choose to have the men read the corresponding *Sleeping Giant* trade book as well. This is optional. If you opt in, have them read chapters 1-4 before the first Core Team meeting.

Pastor, this Core Team of men will have your back and will lift up your arms as you begin an intentional effort to help the men of your community and congregation Get In, Get Healthy, Get Strong, and Get Going into the mission of the church. You might consider meeting informally over coffee or lunch to pass out the books and cast vision for this training in intentional men's ministry. You may also arrange a time when the men can view Kenny's message to the church on the DVD as a way to prime the pump and generate enthusiasm. Have Core Team members sign the covenant found on page 156.

FINDING YOUR CORE TEAM

The Core Team is a group of men whom God has already called to help you raise up and train the next generation of men. They will be the leadership engine that consistently reaches and reproduces strong men for church needs and initiatives. You will want to spend time praying for God to reveal whom He has called. These men will be the models for the men you'd like to see step out churchwide.

SESSION 01 // WAITING FOR A HERO

In this session Kenny teaches about the cultural oppression that slumbering men produce in their families, communities, churches, and nations. You will want to rally this Core Team of men to reject a culture of passivity and boldly step into God's kingdom purpose for their lives so that they can lead the men of the church to do the same.

Review (10-15 min.) Questions are provided to help members share from their Work at Home study. Feel free to review other questions instead or allow men to share more of their personal goals for this training if you sense God's leadership to modify the group time.

Watch Video Session 1: "Waiting for a Hero" (29:00)

- The <u>behaviors</u> of men are at the center of most suffering.
- Broken male culture is the <u>wallpaper</u> of modern journalism.
- Men are being called by God into a movement of <u>spirituality</u> and <u>justice</u>.
- The hope of the world is the local <u>church</u>.
- If the men of our churches are not <u>healthy</u>, the churches are not <u>healthy</u>.

Video Feedback (15 min.) Review your notes from the video teaching and have group members share using the questions provided. It is important for the men to be able to unpack what they have heard from Kenny and apply the truths to their lives in your Core Team's context.

Activity: Church and Parachurch: A Marriage Made in Heaven (20-30 min.) This small-group activity is designed to help your Core Team understand its men's ministry context, particularly as it relates to events and/or parachurch ministries that have either aided or distracted from your church's vision. If your Core Team has more than five men, break into groups of two or three to discuss the questions. Then discuss together with the Core Team.

Bible Study (30 min.) These questions will facilitate discussion and help men further apply principles from God's Word to their lives. Encourage men to share their stories as a source of encouragement to other members of the Core Team as you build a biblical foundation for intentional men's ministry.

Wrap (5 min.) Restate the main teaching points and remind men of tasks to accomplish for next week. Especially encourage them to complete their Work at Home study before the next meeting. Close in prayer.

SESSION 02 // A MOVEMENT BEGINS WITH A MAN

In this session Kenny teaches about God's pattern for men to be the chief influencers and agents of His plans in this world. You will want to remind the Core Team of their important role as influencers so that God's pattern of leadership can be multiplied throughout the church.

Review (10-15 min.) Questions are provided to help members share from their Work at Home study. Feel free to review other questions instead or allow men to share testimonies from the previous week if you sense God's leadership to modify the group time.

Watch Video Session 2: "A Movement Begins with a Man" (26:00)

- Your attitude about men reflects your ministry to men.
- The church all over the world is struggling to deliver its mission unnecessarily.
- Jesus started with men.
- Job one for Jesus: Start calling men and fully train them.
- Jesus Christ practiced intentional men's ministry.

Video Feedback (15 min.) Review your notes from the video teaching and have group members share using the questions provided. It is important for the men to be able to unpack what they have heard from Kenny and apply the truths to their lives in your Core Team's context.

Activity: Vineyard of Hope (20-30 min.) This small-group activity is designed to help your Core Team capture the vision and further understand the biblical principles necessary for an effective men's ministry. If your

Core Team has more than five men, break into smaller groups of two or three to discuss the questions. Then discuss together with the Core Team.

Bible Study (30 min.) These questions will facilitate discussion and help men further apply principles from God's Word to their lives. Encourage men to share their stories as a source of encouragement to other members of the Core Team as you build a biblical foundation for intentional men's ministry.

Wrap (5 min.) Restate the main teaching points from this session and remind the men of tasks to accomplish for next week. Especially encourage them to complete their Work at Home study before the next meeting. Close in prayer.

SESSION 03 // MISSION, VISION, AND ALIGNMENT

In this session Kenny teaches about the necessity of a strong mission and vision for your men's ministry and the importance of alignment with the senior pastor's overall vision for the church. You will want to remind the Core Team of just how significant they are in making this happen.

Review (10-15 min.) Questions are provided to help members share from their Work at Home study. Feel free to review other questions instead or allow men to share testimonies from the previous week if you sense God's leadership to modify the group time.

Watch Video Session 3: "Mission, Vision, and Alignment" (31:00)

• Churches often don't know what the <u>target</u> for men's ministry is.
• A good vision and mission statement motivates people <u>internally</u>.
• A good vision and mission statement <u>rallies</u> resources.
• The pastor's <u>success</u> is your <u>success</u>.
• The men in your church want to be seen as <u>integral</u> in the life of the church.

Video Feedback (15 min.) Review your notes from the video teaching and have group members share using the questions provided. It is important for the men to be able to unpack what they have heard from Kenny and apply the truths to their lives in your Core Team's context.

Activity: Magic Wand, Part 1 (20-30 min.) This small-group activity is designed to help your Core Team begin developing a strong mission and vision statement for your church's men's ministry. End-visioning is a great place to start and the magic wand question will help you do that. If your Core Team has more than five men, break into smaller groups of two or three to discuss the questions. Then discuss together with the Core Team. Listing your ideas on a whiteboard will help the Core Team process together.

Bible Study (30 min.) These questions will facilitate discussion and help men further apply principles from God's Word to their lives. Encourage men to share their stories as a source of encouragement to other members of the Core Team as you build a biblical foundation for intentional men's ministry.

Wrap (5 min.) Restate the main teaching points and remind men of tasks to accomplish for next week. Especially encourage them to complete their Work at Home study before the next meeting. They should also bring with them their ideas for a targeted mission and vision statement. Close in prayer.

SESSION 04 // STRONG FUNNELS AND PATHWAYS

In this session Kenny teaches about the powerful funnels needed to draw men into meaningful men's ministry and the spiritual pathways necessary to keep them. You will want to remind the Core Team of how important it is for them to go through this process and to lead by example.

Review (10-15 min.) Questions are provided to help members share from their Work at Home study. Feel free to review other questions instead or allow men to share testimonies from the previous week if you sense God's leadership to modify the group time.

Watch Video Session 4: "Strong Funnels and Pathways" (31:00)

• Strong <u>funnels</u> call out to those urgent needs that men are facing.
• Men are masters of <u>self-protection</u> and <u>self-preservation</u>.
• The four steps on the spiritual pathway for men are "Get <u>In</u>," "Get <u>Healthy</u>," "Get <u>Strong</u>," and "Get <u>Going</u>."
• The goal of "Get Strong" is an aggressive spiritual expression of the <u>Great</u> <u>Commandment</u> and the <u>Great</u> <u>Commission</u>.

Video Feedback (15 min.) Review your notes from the video teaching and have group members share using the questions provided. It is important for the men to be able to unpack what they have heard from Kenny and apply the truths to their lives in your Core Team's context.

Activity: Magic Wand, Part 2 (20-30 min.) This activity is designed to help your Core Team consolidate their work from the previous week and walk away with a clear vision and mission statement. Listing your ideas on a whiteboard will help the Core Team process together. If you feel you need more time, you might consider scheduling a retreat at the end of your *Sleeping Giant* experience.

Bible Study (30 min.) These questions will facilitate discussion and help men further apply principles from God's Word to their lives. Encourage men to share their stories as a source of encouragement to other members of the Core Team as you build a biblical foundation for intentional men's ministry.

Wrap (5 min.) Restate the main teaching points and remind men of tasks to accomplish for next week. Especially encourage them to complete their Work at Home study before the next meeting. Close in prayer.

SESSION 05 // STRONG RELATIONAL CORE AND GROUPS

In this session Kenny teaches about the strong relational core needed to keep men and men's ministry energized. He also stresses the small-group emphasis necessary to sustain a vibrant men's ministry. You will want to remind the Core Team of the important role they play as the foundation of this structure.

Review (10-15 min.) Questions are provided to help members share from their Work at Home study. Feel free to review other questions instead or allow men to share testimonies from the previous week if you sense God's leadership to modify the group time.

Watch Video Session 5: "Strong Relational Core and Groups" (33:00)

- A strong relationship infrastructure drives an effective men's ministry and gives it meaning.
- There is no such thing as a strong but relationally shallow men's ministry.
- Authentic relational deposits bring powerful relational capital that you can spend on strategic "asks."
- A strong relational dynamic in the men's ministry starts with the pastor and Core Team.
- The church must have one message to the men and one place for them to start the process.

Video Feedback (15 min.) Review your notes from the video teaching and have group members share using the questions provided. It is important for the men to be able to unpack what they have heard from Kenny and apply the truths to their lives in your Core Team's context.

Activity: Problems That Groups Solve (20-30 min.) This small-group activity is designed to help your Core Team think through your current structure and consider how men's groups can be implemented. If your Core Team has more than five men, break into smaller groups of two or three to discuss the principles. Then discuss together.

Bible Study (30 min.) These questions will facilitate discussion and help men further apply principles from God's Word to their lives. Encourage men to share their stories as a source of encouragement to other members of the Core Team as you build a biblical foundation for intentional men's ministry.

Wrap (5 min.) Restate the main teaching points and remind men of tasks to accomplish for next week. Especially encourage them to complete their Work at Home study before the next meeting, including the *Sleeping Giant* Assessment, Part 1. Close in prayer.

SESSION 06 // "GO" TIME

In this session Kenny illustrates how to implement the *Sleeping Giant* process using different church scenarios. You will want to remind the Core Team that the men of the church will need to trust in their leadership and the process if every man is truly to be a minister in your church and community. It's "Go" time!

Review (10-15 min.) Questions are provided to help members share from their Work at Home study. Feel free to review other questions instead or allow men to share testimonies from the previous week if you sense God's leadership to modify the group time.

Watch Video Session 6: "'Go' Time" (28:00)

• Your men's ministry must have the <u>breadth</u> and <u>width</u> to meet any man that encounters it with meaning and in context.
• The *Sleeping Giant* process makes every man a <u>minister</u> and invites him into the <u>priesthood</u> of believers.
• The men have to know that your <u>culture</u> and your <u>process</u> are rock solid.

Video Feedback (15 min.) Review your notes from the video teaching and have group members share using the questions provided. It is important for the men to be able to unpack what they have heard from Kenny and apply the truths to their lives in your Core Team's context.

Activity: *Sleeping Giant* Assessment, Part 2 (45-60 min.) This activity is designed to help your Core Team determine where your men's ministry is at present and what pathway you will need to follow to implement the *Sleeping Giant* process. Listing your ideas on a whiteboard will help the Core Team process together. You may need to schedule more time to plan your calendar for implementation, perhaps a Saturday morning or a full weekend retreat. You will notice there is no Bible Study in this session since the biblical foundation has been laid. Prayerfully plan during this work session and apply the biblical principles you have learned. There is a worksheet included in this Leader Guide where you can compile or transfer your work.

Wrap (5 min.) Restate the main teaching points from this lesson and encourage the men as you move on together on the *Sleeping Giant* pathway. You will want to schedule your start date for Get Healthy with the Core Team before you leave. Close in prayer.

NEXT STEPS

Your Core Team is now prepared for the Get Healthy stage on the *Sleeping Giant* pathway. This begins with the 8-week study *Temptation*. From there, you should stay together to study *Intimacy, Family,* and *Friendship* before moving on to the Get Strong stage. Once there, you may begin planning "Get In" catalytic events and leading Get Healthy groups among the men of your church.

Be sure to register your church at **everymanministries.com/registration**. You will then receive a confirmation e-mail. Registration will allow you to receive our newsletter and support from our coaching network. You will be contacted within two weeks by a *Sleeping Giant* coach who can answer questions and guide you in a successful launch to your men's ministry.

Worksheet

VISION:

MISSION:

PATHWAY STRATEGY (CATALYTIC EVENTS AND SPIRITUAL PATHWAY IMPLEMENTATION):

What Does a Successful Men's Ministry Look Like?

Far from a "program" or another Bible study to begin and complete, LifeWay presents to churches men's ministry tools that get men on a spiritual pathway. These tools take the men in your church on a journey to greater spiritual maturity in becoming better husbands, fathers, and workers. Any effective men's ministry begins with the pastor and his vision. Because we cannot be effective ministers in a vacuum, we recommend the pastor recruit a Core Team of men to prayerfully walk through this process with him.

We believe that any significant men's ministry begins with a catalytic event that (1) motivates men; (2) shares a vision; and (3) gets men into groups. The *Courageous Bible Study* may serve as a catalytic event for your men's ministry and may already be in motion. Other events that we've seen work effectively are men's retreats in their various forms, Kenny Luck conferences, and other opportunities such as wild game dinners and banquets.

The catalytic event gets men onto a spiritual pathway that begins with spiritual health before transitioning to spiritual strength and finally into greater service and missionality. In partnership with Kenny Luck and Every Man Ministries, LifeWay advocates a spiritual pathway for men with the following key stages:

GET MEN IN typically utilizes a catalytic event. It should come as no surprise that your ministry to men begins with an event that draws men and gives you an initial opportunity to share the vision that the pastor and the Core Team have created. This event generates excitement within the men of your church.

GET MEN HEALTHY is the first step on the spiritual pathway that relies on a small-group experience. Each resource in this stage addresses a key issue in the life of the men in your church. Written by experienced practitioners, these small-group studies examine issues like temptation, friendship, leading a family, and understanding a woman's heart.

GET MEN STRONG Once a man has confronted the core issues identified in getting spiritually healthy, he continues on the pathway to Get Strong. These small-group experiences build on the foundation laid in the first two stages. The pathway we recommend begins with Kenny Luck's *Risk*. This 8-week group experience takes men to the proverbial "next level" discipleship and helps them say goodbye to playing it safe and to start radically trusting Jesus.

GET MEN GOING Once healthy and strong, men on the spiritual pathway are ready to Get Going. Get Going can include a number of actions like leading other men as they engage the spiritual pathway, choosing missional opportunities offered by your church or other organizations, or greater involvement in ongoing church ministries.

How to Host a Catalytic Event: Get In

The first funnel in your spiritual pathway is the catalytic event that (1) motivates men; (2) shares a vision; and (3) gets men into groups. Because many ministries offer inspiration without progression, your catalytic event should offer the former without sacrificing the latter. More than likely your church is already hosting catalytic events or could easily create one.

HERE ARE SOME IDEAS:

- Show a movie like *Courageous* or *Facing the Giants.* For details go to *www.lifeway.com/films.*
- Host a *RISK* conference (*www.everymanministries.com*).
- Plan a tailgating party in the fall or spring.
- Offer a "beast feast" or wild game dinner.
- Host a *Game Plan for Life* simulcast or other event during NFL or NASCAR season (*www.lifeway.com/gameplan*).
- Take advantage of a church campaign for a special "call out" to the men of your church.
- Plan a retreat for the men of your church. Depending on the size of your church, you may choose a special on-site event or something away from your facility.

HERE ARE THE STEPS FOR HOSTING AN EVENT:

1. Choose a date and a venue. Pray for this event.
2. Invite a team to plan, design, and customize your event.
3. Four weeks in advance, select a key speaker or host for the event. Include a testimony from one of your men. Gather any supplies you will need, i.e., film, projector, chairs, tables, etc.
4. Three weeks in advance, decide on food and decorations. Begin promoting your event using the publicity tools provided in the *Sleeping Giant Leader Kit.*
5. Two weeks in advance, follow up with any planning details and continue taking advantage of any and all marketing outlets.
6. One week in advance, check in with presenters. Confirm your food and decorations and solidify any necessary event volunteers.
7. Implement your event.
8. Be sure to have a table for Get Healthy sign-ups. You will want to communicate in multiple ways and often that Get Healthy is the next step on the pathway for men who attend your Get In event. Really encourage men from the church and community to get in a group.

How to Implement the Pathway:
Get Healthy + Get Strong

We have said before that one of the strengths of the *Sleeping Giant* model is that you don't have to tear down your existing structure in order to implement the pathway. However, you do have to make room within your structure. This may require an extra time commitment from your men, but guys, this is worth it. Below are some suggestions for implementing the pathway. Remember, no one knows your context better than you, so feel free to modify these suggestions.

IF YOUR CHURCH USES SUNDAY SCHOOL AS YOUR PRIMARY INSTRUCTIONAL AND FELLOWSHIP MODEL:
1. Have your **men's classes** schedule an 8-week Get Healthy or Get Strong study each semester.
2. Have your **couple's classes** plan to divide into a men's and women's class structure periodically.
3. Have your **men in couple's classes** meet for an additional hour during the week at someone's home or at a restaurant for your Get Healthy or Get Strong studies as often as you would like.

If your church has an additional time set aside each week for short-term **DISCIPLESHIP TRAINING**, perhaps on Sunday or Wednesday evenings, consider planning a men's spiritual pathway track that men can follow as they Get Healthy and Get Strong. Depending on the size of your church, you could have several studies within that track running concurrently.

IF YOUR CHURCH USES SMALL GROUPS AS YOUR PRIMARY INSTRUCTIONAL AND FELLOWSHIP MODEL:
1. Have your **men's small groups** schedule an 8-week Get Healthy or Get Strong study 2-3 times per year or stay with it until your groups have been through all of these studies.
2. Have your **couple's small groups** plan to divide into a men's and women's group structure periodically. This could be in separate rooms at the same house or at different homes depending on your childcare arrangements.
3. Have your **men in couple's small groups** meet for an additional hour during the week at someone's home or at a restaurant for your Get Healthy or Get Strong studies as often as you would like.

LEADERSHIP: Consider using the *Sleeping Giant* pathway as your primary means for leadership training for men in the church. This could be staff, deacons, or elders as well as lay leaders of other ministries in the church. As these men Get Healthy, Get Strong, and Get Going, you will want to help them lead other men along the pathway as well, probably through one of the means above.

Welcome to Community!

Meeting together to study God's Word and experience life together is an exciting adventure. A small group is a group of people unwilling to settle for anything less than redemptive community.

CORE VALUES

COMMUNITY: God is relational, so He created us to live in relationship with Him and each other. Authentic community involves sharing life together and connecting on many levels with others in our Core Team.

GROUP PROCESS: Developing authentic community takes time. It's a journey of sharing our stories with each other and learning together. Every healthy group goes through stages over a period of months or years. We begin with the birth of a new group, then deepen our relationships in the growth and development stages.

INTERACTIVE BIBLE STUDY: God gave the Bible as our instruction manual for life. We need to deepen our understanding of God's Word. People learn and remember more as they wrestle with truth and learn from others. Bible discovery and group interaction enhance growth.

EXPERIENTIAL GROWTH: Beyond solely reading, studying, and dissecting the Bible, being a disciple of Christ involves reunifying knowledge with experience. We do this by taking questions to God, opening a dialogue with our hearts (instead of killing desire), and utilizing other ways to listen to God speak (other people, nature, art, movies, circumstances). Experiential growth is always grounded in the Bible as God's primary revelation and our ultimate truth-source.

POWER OF GOD: Processes and strategies will be ineffective unless we invite and embrace the presence and power of God. In order to experience community and growth, Jesus needs to be the centerpiece of our group experiences and the Holy Spirit must be at work.

REDEMPTIVE COMMUNITY: Healing best occurs within the context of community and relationships. It's vital to see ourselves through the eyes of others, share our stories, and ultimately find freedom from the secrets and lies that enslave our souls.

MISSION: God has invited us into a larger story with a great mission of setting captives free and healing the brokenhearted (Isaiah 61:1-2). However, we can only join in this mission to the degree that we've let Jesus bind up our wounds and set us free. Others will be attracted to an authentic redemptive community.

SHARING YOUR STORIES

The sessions of the *Sleeping Giant Core Team Workbook* are designed to help you share a bit of your personal life with the other people in your group as you experience life together. Through your time together, each member of the Core Team is encouraged to move from low risk, less personal sharing to higher risk communication. Real community will not develop apart from increasing intimacy over time.

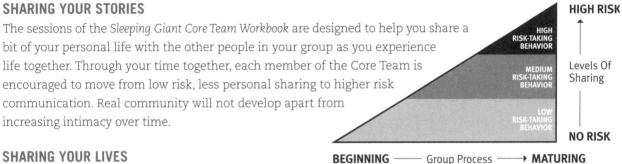

SHARING YOUR LIVES

As you share your lives together during this time, it's important to recognize that it's God who brought each person to this Core Team, gifting the individuals to play a vital role in the group (1 Corinthians 12:1). Each of you was uniquely designed to contribute in your own unique way to building into the lives of the other people in your group. As you get to know one another better, consider the following four areas that will be unique for each person. These areas will help you get a "grip" on how you can better support others and how they can support you.

G - SPIRITUAL GIFTS:

   God has given you unique spiritual gifts (1 Corinthians 12; Romans 12:3-8; Ephesians 4:1-16).

R - RESOURCES:

   You have resources that perhaps only you can share, including skill, abilities, possessions, money, and time (Acts 2:44-47; Ecclesiastes 4:9-12).

I - INDIVIDUAL EXPERIENCES:

   You have past experiences, both good and bad, that God can use to strengthen and encourage others (2 Corinthians 1:3-7; Romans 8:28).

P - PASSIONS:

   There are things that excite and motivate you. God has given you those desires and passions to use for His purposes (Psalm 37:4,23; Proverbs 3:5-6,13-18).

To better understand how a group should function and develop in these four areas, consider taking your Core Team on a journey in community using the LifeWay Small Groups study entitled *Great Beginnings*.

Leading a Small Group

You will find a great deal of helpful information in this section that will be crucial for success as you lead your group.

Reading through this section and utilizing the suggested principles and practices will greatly enhance the group experience. First is to accept the limitations of leadership. You cannot transform a life. You must lead your group to the Bible, the Holy Spirit, and the power of Christian community. By doing so your group will have all the tools necessary to draw closer to God and to each other, and to experience heart transformation.

MAKE THE FOLLOWING THINGS AVAILABLE AT EACH SESSION:

+ *Sleeping Giant Core Team Workbook* for each attendee
+ Extra Bibles
+ Snacks and refreshments (encourage everyone to bring something)
+ Pens or pencils for each attendee

THE SETTING AND GENERAL TIPS

#1 Prepare for each meeting by reviewing the material, praying for each group member, asking the Holy Spirit to join you, and making Jesus the centerpiece of every experience.

#2 Create the right environment by making sure chairs are arranged so each person can see every other attendee. Set the room temperature at 69 degrees. If meeting in a home, make sure pets are where they cannot interrupt the meeting. Request that cell phones be turned off unless someone is expecting an emergency call.

#3 Try to have soft drinks and coffee available for early arrivals.

#4 Have someone ready to make the men feel welcome as they arrive.

#5 Be sure there is adequate lighting so that everyone can read without straining.

#6 Think of ways to connect with team members away from Core Team time. The amount of participation you have during your Core Team meetings is directly related to the amount of time you connect with your team members away from the Core Team meeting. Consider sending e-mails, texts, or social networking messages during the week encouraging them to come next week and to expect God to do great things throughout the course of this study.

#7 There are four types of questions used in each session: Observation (What is the passage telling us?), Interpretation (What does the passage mean?), Self-revelation (How am I doing in light of the truth unveiled?), and Application (Now that I know what I know, what will I do to integrate this truth into my life?). You won't be able to use all the questions in each study, but be sure to use some from each.

#8 Don't lose patience about the depth of relationship group members are experiencing. Building authentic Christian community takes time.

#9 Be sure pens or pencils are available for attendees at each meeting.

#10 Never ask someone to pray aloud without first asking their permission.

LEADING MEETINGS

#1 Before the Review sections, do not say, "Now we're going to do a review." The entire session should feel like a conversation from beginning to end, not a classroom experience.

#2 Be certain every member responds to the Review questions. The goal is for every person to hear his or her own voice early in the meeting. People will then feel comfortable to converse later on. If members can't think of a response, let them know you'll come back to them after the others have spoken.

#3 Remember, a great group leader talks less than 10 percent of the time. If you ask a question and no one answers, just wait. If you create an environment where you fill the gaps of silence, the group will quickly learn they don't need to join you in the conversation.

#4 Don't be hesitant to call people by name as you ask them to respond to questions or to give their opinions. Be sensitive, but engage everyone in the conversation.

#5 Don't call on people to read aloud unless you have gotten their permission prior to the meeting. Feel free to ask for volunteers to read.

#6 Watch your time. If discussion extends past the time limits suggested, offer the option of pressing on into other discussions or continuing the current content into your next meeting.

REMEMBER: People and their needs are always more important than completing your agenda or finishing all the questions.

LifeWay has pulled together the perfect dream team to help you become the man that God wants you to be. It includes proven champions in the sports world and leading thinkers in men's ministry—people like **Joe Gibbs**, **Tony Dungy**, **Kenny Luck**, and **Tony Evans**.

LifeWay | Men

We also offer a daily devotional, which you can learn about at lifeway.com/standfirm, and the free Stand Firm Webshow at lifeway.com/men. Visit the links below to see even more ways we're supporting and encouraging Christian men.

(b) lifeway.com/powerofthehome

(f) facebook.com/lifewaymen

(t) twitter.com/lifewaymen

(v) vimeo.com/lifewaymen

w w w . l i f e w a y . c o m / m e n

LifeWay | Me

Want to get something started at your church?

All you need is a little Luck.

If you're going to follow the *Sleeping Giant* model and host a "Get In" event, why not invite the very creator of that model to be your main speaker? Kenny Luck will come to your event with a strong, challenging message that will naturally lead your men into the next stage of "Get Healthy." But watch out! He may just start a revolution that will impact your men, their marriages, and your overall leadership. Visit us online for more information.

everymanministries.com/events

LifeWay | Men

Core Team Covenant

As you begin this study, it is important that your Core Team covenant together, agreeing to live out important group values. Once these values are agreed upon, your Core Team will be on its way to experiencing true Christian community. It's very important that your Core Team discuss these values—preferably as you begin this study. The first session would be most appropriate.

PRIORITY: While we are in this group, we will give the Core Team meetings priority.

PARTICIPATION: Everyone is encouraged to participate and no one dominates.

RESPECT: Everyone is given the right to his own opinions, and all questions are encouraged and respected.

CONFIDENTIALITY: Anything that is said in our meetings is never repeated outside the meeting without permission.

LIFE CHANGE: We will regularly assess our progress toward applying the "steps" to an amazing life passionately following Christ.

CARE AND SUPPORT: Permission is given to call upon each other at any time, especially in times of crisis. The group will provide care for every member.

ACCOUNTABILITY: We agree to let the members of our Core Team hold us accountable to commitments we make in whatever loving ways we decide upon. Unsolicited advice-giving is not permitted.

MISSION: We agree as a Core Team to work toward multiplication of our group to form new groups.

MINISTRY: We will encourage one another to volunteer to serve in a ministry and to support missions work by giving financially and/or personally serving.

I, _____, agree to all of the above.   Date: _____

Core Team Directory

Write your name on this page. Pass your books around and ask Core Team members to fill in their names and contact information in each other's books.

YOUR NAME: _____

Name: _____
Home Phone: _____
Mobile Phone: _____
E-mail: _____
Social Network(s): _____

Name: _____
Home Phone: _____
Mobile Phone: _____
E-mail: _____
Social Network(s): _____

Name: _____
Home Phone: _____
Mobile Phone: _____
E-mail: _____
Social Network(s): _____

Name: _____
Home Phone: _____
Mobile Phone: _____
E-mail: _____
Social Network(s): _____

Name: _____
Home Phone: _____
Mobile Phone: _____
E-mail: _____
Social Network(s): _____

Name: _____
Home Phone: _____
Mobile Phone: _____
E-mail: _____
Social Network(s): _____

Name: _____
Home Phone: _____
Mobile Phone: _____
E-mail: _____
Social Network(s): _____

Name: _____
Home Phone: _____
Mobile Phone: _____
E-mail: _____
Social Network(s): _____

Name: _____
Home Phone: _____
Mobile Phone: _____
E-mail: _____
Social Network(s): _____

Name: _____
Home Phone: _____
Mobile Phone: _____
E-mail: _____
Social Network(s): _____

Name: _____
Home Phone: _____
Mobile Phone: _____
E-mail: _____
Social Network(s): _____

Name: _____
Home Phone: _____
Mobile Phone: _____
E-mail: _____
Social Network(s): _____